"HERE, THE PEOPLE RULE"

"Here, the People Rule"

— Y —

A Constitutional Populist Manifesto

RICHARD D. PARKER

Harvard University Press

Cambridge, Massachusetts
London, England
1994

Library of Congress Cataloging-in-Publication Data
Parker, Richard, 1945–
   "Here, the people rule": a constitutional populist
manifesto/Richard Parker.
     p.   cm.
   "Revised version of the Seegars Lecture given in October 1992
at the Valparaiso University School of Law and published in 27
Valparaiso University law review 531 (1993)"—Pref.
     ISBN 0-674-38925-5 (cloth: acid-free paper)
     ISBN 0-674-38926-3 (pbk.: acid-free paper)
   1. Representative government and representation.
   2. Majorities. 3. Minorities. 4. Democracy. 5. Populism.
   6. Constitutional law. I. Title.
JF1051.P29 1994
321.8—dc20   94-2387
          CIP

This is a revised version of the Seegars Lecture given in October 1992 at the Valparaiso University School of Law and published in 27 *Valparaiso University Law Review* 531 (1993).

The title "Here, the People Rule" is taken from the remarks of Gerald Ford upon taking the oath of office as President—just after waving goodbye to Richard Nixon—on August 9, 1974.

Actually, another date more deeply touches this manifesto. On June 5, 1968, when Bobby Kennedy was killed, ordinary people in America were left without a leader—on our own, as, in truth, we ought to be.

CONTENTS

Introduction   1

I. Political Energy   7

II. "Higher" Law?   51

Notes   117

"HERE, THE PEOPLE RULE"

INTRODUCTION

V

L ET ME BEGIN at the end. I want to give you some sense of where I'm going. Then, you'll begin to see where I'm coming from.

I'm going to challenge three basic ideas—three connected orthodoxies—central to conventional discourse about constitutional law. They are:

(1) The idea that we must define constitutional democracy as *opposed* to populist democracy: that constitutional constraints on public power in a democracy are meant to contain or tame the exertion of popular political energy rather than to nurture, galvanize, and release it.

(2) The related idea that constitutional law is "higher" law, its substance and process superior to "ordinary" law and politics not just functionally, but (somehow) in essential quality as well.

(3) The consequent idea that the main mission of modern constitutional law is to stand "above

3

the battle" so as to protect "individuals" and "minorities" against the ruling "majority."

I am going to urge, in fact, that constitutional law should be devoted as much—and even more—to *promote* majority rule as to *limit* it.

To challenge such basic ideas, I've got to go to the root of the matter. But what *is* the root of the matter? It is, I believe, a matter of sensibility. It involves our assumptions, imagination, and attitudes—assumptions about, imagination of, and attitudes toward the political energy of ordinary people. For that is the kernel of democracy, of a regime in which offices are open to ordinary citizens and in which ordinary people are allowed, and even expected, to act collectively to influence, and even control, the government. After all, democracy—its aspirations, its operation, its dangers—is what, most fundamentally, our Constitution is *about*.

My starting point—I won't defend it here,[1] but will just start from it—is this: Our attitudes toward the political energy of ordinary people shape our sense of what are the constitutive problems of our democracy. Thus, these attitudes shape our notions of what should be the mission of constitutional law.

That, in turn, shapes our ideas about the appropriate substance of constitutional principles and the proper form of reasoning about their derivation, definition, and application. And that, in turn, shapes our views about the nature and legitimacy of active judicial review in the name of the Constitution. Taken altogether, then, I start from the proposition that attitudes toward ordinary people as active, energetic participants, collectively and singly, in politics and government operate both to animate and to structure our whole discourse about constitutional law.

How to get at something so slippery, so invisible, as sensibility? How, even, to talk about it? The approach least likely to self-destruct from the outset is an indirect one, a tentative one, respectful of the deeply controversial and dubious status of anything said about the matter. I won't pretend to "prove" or "demonstrate" anything. Instead, I'll adopt the strategy of a sermon—the sort of sermon, at any rate, I remember hearing as a child in the Unitarian Church. To start, I'll try to inspire you to inspect and to question both your own sensibility and general attitudes you discern "in the air" of our legal and political culture. Only after that will I be more openly didactic.

I

POLITICAL ENERGY

V

I F WHAT IS at stake is a sensibility, it seems to me that the most fruitful approach to it might be through a work of fiction. When easing into any sensitive territory, a traditional move, after all, is to turn to a story.

The story I've chosen is *Mario and the Magician*,[2] written in 1929 by Thomas Mann. But you ask: Why that one, more than half a century old, by a German, set in the Italy of Mussolini? My reason is straightforward. It is "about" politics. Though Mussolini is barely mentioned in it, it's widely understood as being, specifically, about the rise of fascism. The editor of a recent anthology of short fiction describes it as a "fictional exploration of the dynamics of fascism in Mussolini's Italy."[3] But what has it to do with *our* politics? The fascist episode, I believe, is still relatively vivid in our imagination. More important, it evokes what appear to me to be some of our deepest, most problematic attitudes about the nature and peril of popular political energy in our own democracy—attitudes to which the story, then, gives us access.

Getting at a "legal" sensibility through a work of fiction, nevertheless, has its pitfalls and so depends on respect for a couple of ground rules. First, we have to keep in mind our purpose in considering this story. Like any other work of fiction, *Mario and the Magician* can be approached from all sorts of angles; doing anything like full justice to it would involve considering all of them.[4] Doing full justice to the story, however, is not the point here. Our focus must be fixed on the issue at hand: the issue of political sensibility. Second, we should avoid entanglement in arguments about competing "methods" of interpretation. When lawyers, in particular, confront a text, they tend to look for its "meaning"—they assume it should have one, most plausible meaning—and they get hung up on issues of proper techniques or criteria for identifying that meaning. Thus, approaching fiction, they tend to worry over the intent of the author, his other works and general views, the "real" historical-social context, and so forth. But, for our purpose, none of this matters. We can forget about such external criteria of meaning. For the meaning of the text—its "correct" interpretation—is not what we are after. What we are after is, rather, our own reaction to the story. In that reaction, we seek insight into a sensibility.

So, the question to ask is: What do we make of the story? That involves: What sensibility does it engage, what attitudes does it evoke, in us? And that implicates a question that will occupy us most: What is it in the story that works to evoke our reaction? What elements in it do we notice and stress? How do we envision them coming together? What pattern do we see? The idea, in other words, is to use the story as a sort of Rorschach ink blot test. What we are seeking might be called a "reading" of the story. But since that may sound too fancy, let's just ask: What is our "take" on it?

In fact, I'm going to sketch not just one take on *Mario and the Magician*, but two. They are different, involving opposed attitudes toward the political energy and activity of ordinary people, opposed sensibilities. Though our appreciation of the story will benefit if we recognize both, that is not easy to do. Most readers tend to see one first, resonating more harmoniously to it, maybe having to struggle to see the other at all. In this respect, the story works not simply as an ink blot test, but as the familiar kind of "reversible figure" sketch found in basic psychology texts:[5] Our eye perceives it as a duck *or* a rabbit, as an old woman *or* a young woman; the patterns are opposed, so it is hard to see both at once; one tends to assume priority. Later, I'll suggest that the first of the "takes" on Thomas Mann's story tends to assume a similar priority in our minds. The second—being distinctly secondary—I'll call a "double take."

Now, let's turn to the story. It has two parts. In the first part, consuming about a third of the whole, the narrator—Northern European, apparently upper middle class—arrives in August to vacation in Torre di Venere, a small resort town on the Italian coast. With him are his wife and two young children. They stay a few days in the Grand Hotel and then move to a smaller pensione. They endure unpleasant episodes on the beach. In the second part, the narrator and his family go to what is advertised as a magic show by a man named Cipolla. The rest of the story is about the show. It turns out that Cipolla is a hypnotist adept at manipulating people from his audience. His manipulation becomes more and more intrusive and humiliating as the show proceeds, finally climaxing in his hypnosis of Mario, a young waiter. Cipolla gets Mario to address him in the name of the woman he loves, and then to kiss him, blissfully, on the cheek. Snapped out of his trance, Mario—horrified—fires a gun at Cipolla. Cipolla crumples to the floor. The narrator and his family move toward the exit. The police arrive. The story ends.

The focus of most readers is on the longer, more florid second part of the story. But, if the story contains any unambiguous instruction for its own reading, it is this: the second part is some sort of echo of the first. Up front—in the very first paragraph—the narrator draws a frame around the story. "From the first moment," he states, "the air of the place made us uneasy . . . then at the end came the shocking business of Cipolla . . . who seemed to incorporate . . . all the evilness of the situation as a whole." An issue that any take on the story will seek to resolve, then, is: What is the relationship between the two parts of the story? What broad pattern do they form? Which is to say: In what does the "evilness of the situation as a whole" consist?[6]

Now, I'm going to sketch one and then the other

take by "telling" the story, emphasizing certain episodes, quoting certain lines, and commenting on certain problems and patterns and attitudes as I go along. Of course, there's no substitute for reading the story yourself—and considering your own reaction to it—before going on to what I have to say. In fact, I urge you stop right here and do just that.

The First "Take"

"The atmosphere of Torre di Venere," begins the narrator, "remains unpleasant in the memory." It "made" him feel "irritable, on edge." From the outset, the focus is on the general, unhealthy condition of the place. This arouses our curiosity: What was wrong with Torre di Venere?

In the next paragraphs, we get an answer. Torre is a place vacationers go to seeking very specific values—"peace," "quiet," a "refuge," an "idyll," a "contemplative," "refined" atmosphere. But, now, such qualities have "ceased to be evident." They are eclipsed by something else—"the world," crowds of people who are "rushing," "seek[ing] peace and put[ting] her to flight." In summer, the crowd "swarms" over the beach. Its "screaming, squabbling, merrymaking"—heightened by "anxious cries" of mothers and "breathy, full-throated" shouts of "pedlars [sic]"—"fill the air." The narrator is under attack. Even the sun "blazing down like mad, peels the skin." But what, exactly, is attacking him? It is: the noise, activity—*energy*—emitted by a crowd. Later, the narrator employs a military metaphor. The "field," he says, was "occupied." By what enemy? He characterizes it simply as "the great public." A mob of "ordinary humanity."[7]

The narrator and his family take up residence in the Grand Hotel. There, two brief episodes ensue. They are similar. Both involve an utterly unreasonable use of power. In both, the narrator is made to suffer. In counterpoint to the "atmosphere" of anxiety—against the background noise of the invasive crowd—these two episodes sharpen the sense of "evil" adumbrated at the start, mixing with the anarchic energy of the mob the kick of arbitrary authority.

The narrator asks, first, to dine in a protected spot, a "cozy nook" out on a veranda "over the water," where "little red-shaded lamps glowed" on the tables. As ever, he is after privacy, peace, and quiet. But he is "informed" that the veranda is reserved

for "clients" of the hotel. This is, of course, non-
sense. The narrator and his family *were* clients,
boarding for several weeks. Without justification,
they are forced to go into the "common light" of the
big dining room, to eat "ordinary and monotonous"
food amidst the crowd.

Shortly thereafter, a favored client in the room
next to the narrator's complains about his child's
coughing, "clinging to the widely held view" that
the condition may be "acoustically contagious." Ac-
cepting this absurd complaint, the manager tells the
narrator to move to "the annexe." The narrator answers unreason with reason. What he gains is the
opportunity to present his case to the hotel physi-
cian. The doctor behaves like an "honest servant of
science." He says there is "no danger of contagion."
Drawing "a long breath," the narrator imagines "the
incident closed." But it is not. The manager dictates
that, despite the medical verdict, they still must move.
The narrator labels this "Byzantinism," a "wilful
breach of faith." It "outraged us," he concludes.[8]

He and his family move to a smaller pensione to
escape the contagion of crowded, overbearing irra-
tionality in the air of the Grand Hotel. He escapes
to find peace: clear boundaries securing individual

autonomy, dignity, and reason. The cozy rooming house has a "clean, cool" dining room where "the service was attentive and good." "[A]ll seemed for the best," says the narrator. "And yet," he continues, "no proper gratification ensued." The sort of peace he seeks is not to be found in Torre. The evil, he complains, "pursued us."

The narrator begins to name the evil: "the naïve misuse of power, the injustice, the sycophantic corruption." He associates it with energy: the light, the heat. He describes "the enormous naïveté of the unrefracted light." He depicts himself assaulted by "[t]he power of the sun . . . so frightful, so relentless." Finally, he portrays what is "pursuing" him in fundamental terms: "collisions with ordinary humanity."

In the heat, the narrator and his family seek relief on the beach and, there, "collisions" escalate. They are "surrounded" by a big crowd of "very average humanity—a middle-class mob" whose aggressive, chaotic noise bombards them. One day, the noise is amplified to an "uproar" when a "repulsive" boy is bitten by a sand-crab. His cries and his mother's "tragic appeals" draw an audience. A doctor—the same one—appears. As a "man of science," he says the boy is not hurt. But the crowd—like the manager of the Grand Hotel—ignores the voice of reason. The boy is "borne off the beach," mob in tow. The next day, he is back, "spoiling our children's sand-castles. Of course, always by accident. . . . [A] perfect terror," says the narrator, under siege.

Finally, the narrator comes "to blows" with his tormentors. His little girl removes her bathing suit on the beach so as to rinse it out. There is an "outburst of anger and resentment" from the crowd. "[W]e became," the narrator notes, "an offence to the public morals." Children hoot and whistle. With "overheated" eloquence, a "gentleman" demands "punitive measures." The basic energy, the "emotionalism of the sense-loving south," mobilizes to insist on "morality and discipline." The narrator answers with calm, polite reason. The mob ignores him. He and his family "must be made an example of." The mob calls on "the authorities." An official pronounces the case *"molto grave."* He commands them to go to the town hall. There, a higher official subjects them to "a stream of the usual didactic phrases—the selfsame tune and words" used earlier by the "gentleman" in the crowd. He confirms the *"molto grave"* verdict. And he levies on them a fine; the narrator calls it a "ransom."

Elements of the story that were in counterpoint are now, in the two incidents on the beach, melded together. At the Grand Hotel, one motif—the energy of the crowds of people "invading" the town—lay, as a backdrop, behind the other—the arbitrary use of power by the hotel management. On the beach, the energy of the crowd lies behind the use of power by town officials in a deeper sense. There is a basic affinity between the two. The crowd's energy seems to fuel, even to generate, the arbitrary exercise of power. When the official exacts a fine from the narrator, his action repeats—in its exaggeration of a trivial event, its obliviousness to reason—the crowd's exaggeration of the sand-crab bite, oblivious to the diagnosis of the doctor. He gives the same speech as the gentleman in the crowd. And, what is more, he demands "ransom" in direct response to the crowd's demand.

Toward the end of the first part of the story, the narrator remarks on the "political" nature of the energy—heated, emotional, ignorant, aggressive, and oppressive—that animates the "ordinary humanity" of the town. He says, "[W]e were in the presence of a national ideal." He views the beach as "alive with patriotic children," and he continues: "There were quarrels over flags, disputes about authority and

⊲

precedence. Grown-ups joined in, not so much to pacify as to render judgment and enunciate principles." Noting that "[p]hrases were dropped about the greatness and dignity of Italy," he identifies the passion of nationalism, of patriotism, as an "illness" spread among the people.[9]

Already, one-third into the story, much of the nightmare of fascism—mass energy arm-in-arm with abuse of power, suppression of disfavored, nonconforming individuals, free-floating pugnacity, all in the name of a group identity—has been enacted. Only the charismatic leader-figure has yet to appear. And he may not be so central after all. For, as the narrator says at the start, he simply "incorporate[d] . . . all the evilness of the situation as a whole."

Now, Cipolla announces himself. Advertising himself, misleadingly, as a mere entertainer, he draws a big audience, all too ready to be drawn in and misled. The people, joined by the narrator and his family, arrive at the hall on time. Cipolla makes them wait, asserting his dominance from the start. When he finally appears, though, he seems not so much to dominate the crowd as to tap into—give vent to—the ill-omened passions that already were agitating it.

The narrator notes not only what is odd in his appearance—"piercing eyes," formal outfit and hunchbacked deformity. He also notices Cipolla's "cross-grained pride," "self-satisfied air," and "energy"—characteristics that he shares with the ordinary people of the town and that thereby begin to intimate the bonds of kinship between him and them. Almost immediately, he mobilizes the energy of the people in a project of subjugation—their own subjugation, something they may have been yearning for secretly, something they are surely suited for. A young man dressed in the "style . . . of the awakened Fatherland"—that is, one of the patriotic mob—speaks up to wish Cipolla a good evening. Cipolla responds, "I like you. . . . People like you are just in my line." Then he continues: "You do what you like. Or is it possible you have ever not done what you liked. . . . What somebody else liked, in short? Hark ye, my friend, that might be a pleasant change for you, to divide up the willing and the doing. . . ." At that, Cipolla tells the young man to stick out his tongue "right down to the roots." The youth resists. Cipolla then makes his claw-handled riding whip "whistle once through the air." The youth shows his tongue. And Cipolla says, "That was me."

Thus boundaries between individuals collapse. The group psychology of the mob gestates its own belligerent will, giving it birth embodied in a leader who turns it back against the people themselves—and the people approve him.

Cipolla, the narrator says, "won his audience." He attributes Cipolla's success partly to his "constant flow of words," operating to "eliminate the gap between stage and audience, which had already been bridged over by the curious skirmish" with the young man. "The mother tongue," he says, is the "national cement." Rhetoric—rather than reason—moves and merges the people. Cipolla's rhetoric reflects to the audience its own personality. The "thin-skinnedness and animosity" of his bluster fascinates them. Cipolla launches into patriotic speeches, echoing the earlier ones by the mob on the beach. When a man, called to the stage, confesses he cannot write, Cipolla calls that "scandalous." "In Italy everybody can write," he proclaims. To "accuse" Italy of harboring an illiterate is to "humiliate the government and the whole country as well." Marking Cipolla's "patriotism" and "irritable sense of dignity," the narrator says that his "countrymen" in the audience felt "in their element with all that."[10]

Twice before the intermission, individuals in the audience challenge Cipolla, each aspiring to assert his "own will." Hypnotically, Cipolla subdues them, his whip cutting the air, leaving one "all but grovell[ing] upon the ground." The narrator feels a "stream of influence" moving not simply from Cipolla to the crowd, but vice versa as well. Cipolla, he feels, acted "in obedience to a voiceless common will" in the air. Cipolla touts his "capacity for self-surrender" to the people, asserting that "[c]ommanding and obeying" are "one indissoluable unity." "[P]eople and leader [are] comprehended in one another," he proclaims. The applause by the audience for Cipolla was, by now, "like a patriotic demonstration."[11]

When, after the intermission, the show resumes, the ugliness of the political energy coursing back and forth between the crowd and Cipolla intensifies. Cipolla launches into "attacks" on autonomy, rationality, morality—many of them "monstrous" and "grotesque"—as the people "laugh and applaud." Hypnotizing the narrator's landlady to leave her husband and come to him, he exhorts the husband to recognize "powers stronger than reason or virtue." Increasingly, he pauses to drink from a glass of liquor, pouring "fuel," says the narrator, upon "his demoniac fires." Intoxicated—and intoxicating—he appeals to the people: "I am the person who is suffering, I am the one to be pitied." The narrator—by now, apparently the only cool head in a febrile mob—notes the peculiarity of eliciting compassion for "a man who is suffering to bring about the humiliation of others."

Building to a climax, Cipolla calls a group to the stage and sets them dancing—"dissolute, abandoned" in "drunken abdication of the critical spirit." A couple of young men volunteer as subjects. An "ecstatic youth" who "gloried in the model facility he had in losing consciousness" falls, at a look, "into a state of military somnambulism," "pleased to be relieved of the burden of voluntary choice." Another, a "gentleman," challenges Cipolla to make him dance. "[Y]our arms and legs are aching for it," Cipolla intones. And, in short order, the man is dancing with his eyes "half shut," a "broad grin" on his face, "having a better time than in his hour of pride." Cipolla's "triumph," the narrator observes, was at "its height," his whip like "Circe's wand"—and, by implication, his audience like Circe's crowd of swine.[12]

At last, Cipolla calls on Mario. He gives Mario the "Roman"—that is, fascist—salute. He feigns tender sympathy for Mario, luring him into shy conversation, trust, vulnerability, and finally intimacy. Tapping the young man's unrequited love for a girl, he speaks in her name, appealing for Mario to express his hidden passion. "Trust me, I love thee. Kiss me here," he says. Mario kisses Cipolla. This is "the moment of Mario's bliss"—"an utter abandonment of the inmost soul, a public exposure of . . . deluded passion and rapture." The narrator characterizes it as "monstrous," "grotesque and thrilling." All protective barriers now seem to be down. Someone in the mob laughs. Cipolla's whip cracks. Mario snaps out of his trance, holds his hands over his "desecrated lips," then he "beat[s] his temples with his clenched fists." He turns and draws a gun. Two shots crash "through applause and laughter." Cipolla collapses, a "heap of clothing, with limbs awry." Chaos ensues. People run to Mario, flinging themselves on him to take away the gun. The narrator calls their behavior, yet again, that of "a mob."

As the police enter, the narrator exits with his family. In the last lines of the story, he sets out his verdict: It was an "end of horror." It was "a liberation." While the mob of ordinary people had no use for, and indeed trampled on, individuality—on reason and virtue, restraint and dignity—one individual did stand apart, one did stand up and so put an "end" to the "horror." Who was it? Was it Mario? An ordinary person pushed farther than the others—his privacy too intimately invaded—who, then, broke loose from the mob? Or was Mario, described as "melancholy," more than ordinary from the start? A romantic, alienated sort of person? A rebel? Or was the individual who stood apart and acted *as* an individual someone else altogether? What of the narrator himself? He most fully embodies reason and virtue. He is the one who keeps a distance not only from Cipolla, but from Cipolla's spiritual kin as well—the people of Torre. Mario's bullets, moreover, will not "end" the real "horror": the "evilness of the situation as a whole." The narrator is the one who grasps that. He gets out of the place. That is the only "end" to the horror. And the only "liberation."[13]

To be sure, power—animated by the fever of the mobilized mass of "average humanity"—has, at the end, been checked. But it took an act of desperation, a violent act. Really, we are safe only if a check by reason on power—by law on the febrile political energy of ordinary people—is built into institutions that give power expression.

That is one take on the story.

The Second "Take"

To shift your perception for a second take—to do a "double take"—on the story, one simple adjustment is required. The adjustment is of a sort perfectly familiar in old-fashioned literary criticism. It involves the status of the narrator. The first take adopts his point of view, empathizing with his sense of the problem, his estimation of "the evilness of the situation as a whole." A second take simply shifts to look at the narrator *as* the problem—as a central part of the "evilness of the situation." That shift produces others, emphasizing different aspects of the story, exposing different patterns in it and evoking very different attitudes toward the political energy of ordinary people.

The opening of the story strikes two notes. One is the dissonant note of "peace" threatened by crowds of vacationers. The other is relatively muffled. It is a note of more personal lament. Specifically, the narrator laments that his young children "had to be present" at "the horrible end of the affair." How is it that the children "had" to be present? He goes on to say that their presence was "due to" Cipolla's false advertising of his show. But should that be the end of the matter? Or does his way of skimming over his own responsibility as a parent suggest, even so early in the story, a passivity—problematic passivity? In his lament, the narrator thus casts suspicion on his desire for "peace." "Luckily," he says, the children did not grasp what went on, so "we let them remain in their happy belief"—their phony peace. Is the "peace" for which the narrator yearns so very different? Or is it, too, a peace of disengagement from the world and the people around him, a peace of passivity?

In the next few paragraphs, the narrator draws three distinctions between himself and the mob crowding into the town. First, he describes them as being "southern," as opposed to his "northern" self. He complains not only of the noise, the "breathy, full-throated southern voice[s]," but also of the "garish" boats, the "repulsive," dusty buses. Second, this rather prissy distinction of the boorish southerner from the more refined northerner plays into a class distinction. The town, he says, was once enjoyed by "the few," but people who "own or rent the villas . . . no longer have . . . their own way" in the place. He feels "temporarily *déclassé*" amid the crowds. And, third, he puts down what he describes as the "national" quality of the vacationing masses—identifying himself, by contrast, as a cosmopolitan, detached from, and superior to, any agglutination of humans. He calls himself a "stranger." And, certainly, his estrangement and his passivity reinforce each other, finding expression in his haughty disdain for the active life of the town, and for the people who lead it.[14]

On second take, what is most remarkable about the events at the Grand Hotel is not the use of power by the management—not its political energy—but the passivity, the *absence* of political energy on the part of the narrator. He turns up his nose at the "ordinary" food and the "common" light in the big dining room, but does not argue when forced to sit there. "[W]e forbore," he remarks, "to press for an explanation." A sign, no doubt, of good breeding. When the manager throws him and his family out of their room, he does argue a bit, but passes the buck to the hotel's doctor. And when the manager ignores the doctor's view, he is "outraged"—what does he then do? He turns tail. "[W]e preferred to leave," he says. He lacks the political energy to engage in a struggle for power. Even more, he seems to disdain it.

Moving to the small pensione, the narrator is content for a time. And what pleases him there? The place, he says, is "cool" and "clean"—isolated from the heat and dirt of the town full of people. In the very same sentence, he remarks that the "service" at the pensione was "attentive and good." Indeed, all he requires from ordinary people, it would appear, is good "service"—and a good distance.

That, of course, is just what he does not get. As he bemoans his "collisions" with ordinary humanity on the beach and complains of the "power" of the sun, he elaborates his basic scorn for the people themselves. He portrays them as "middle class"; "very average"; a "mob." He makes fun of mothers calling their kids: "The voices these women have!" It's not simply the noise that "vex[es]" his "sensitive soul," but the "harsh," "hideously stressed" tones. What impresses him about one child is his "ill-breeding." He calls the boy "repulsive." Even the weather seems to him childish, "dull" and spoiled by an "enormous naïveté" that cannot satisfy his "deeper . . . complex" soul. The "light-heartedness" that it induces among southerners is not for him. He feels "barren" and "a little contemptuous." His contempt inspires a mocking motif that reappears later on. "[I]t is," he says, "classic weather, the sun of Homer, the climate wherein human culture came to flower—and all the rest of it." It amuses him to speak, ironically, of ordinary people and their surroundings in terms of classic antiquity. So, he compares the cries of the "repulsive" boy to "the shout of an antique hero." And, as to the tone of the mothers' voices, he sneers that it was "sometimes hard to believe that we were in the land which is the western cradle of the art of song."[15]

When the narrator proceeds to complain about the patriotism of the people on the beach, his condescension congeals. Imagining them as "just passing through a certain stage, something rather like an illness," he illustrates his penchant to look at the town's adults as children or unruly adolescents. He says that his own children were so "puzzled and hurt" by the people's childish demeanor that they simply "retreat[ed]" from it. But was that not his response as well? Like his children, might not he also be behaving childishly? Another of his condescensions has the same brittle reflexive quality. He scorns the people's "stiffness," their "lack of innocent enjoyment"; they "stood on their dignity," he says. Isn't all that very true, once again, of his own lofty self?

In the conflict over his daughter's lack of a bathing suit, the connections among the narrator's disdain for "average humanity," his "stiff dignity," and his tendency to "puzzled retreat" come to the surface. When the crowd on the beach makes its objection to public nudity, he dismisses this view out of hand. Smugly, he states that "our attitude towards the nude body" has "undergone, all over the world, a fundamental change." The cosmopolitan standard of behavior, valuing "freedom" in the matter, is superior, he assumes, to any local standard. He simply derides the people's attitude as backward and ignorant—attributing it to "emotionalism" and "morality." No wonder, then, that his efforts to answer the crowd on his child's behalf strike no chords. He cannot begin to relate to them. He claims to have had arguments on the tip of his tongue. (Naturally, the "answers" he thought of are haughty, sarcastic put-downs.) But what he comes out with are minimal "mitigating" apologies, offered with irony. He "bow[s] respectfully." And when fined, he says he "paid, and left." He cannot bring himself even to enter the arena, much less put up any kind of fight.

His last word on the episode accentuates the problem: a problem not of invasive energy, but of an *absence* of energy. "Ought we not at this point to have left Torre . . .?" he muses. And he answers himself: "If we only had!" "But," he shrugs feebly, "circumstances combined to prevent us from making up our minds to a change."[16]

What has happened—the story makes clear—is a failure of will. The narrator canvasses a potpourri of rationalizations for it—dignity, curiosity, stoicism, and even indolence. But the critical point is that here, *before* Cipolla comes on the scene, the story shows that it does not take a hypnotist—or fascist leader—to induce a failure of will. What is more, the failure of will established here at the center of the story is not that of ignorant, ordinary people. It is that of one who thinks himself their superior—who mocks their energy; who fears and loathes involvement in any hot, messy, risky political contest; whose own energy is primly embalmed in a refined and elevated dependence upon "rationality" and privacy and peace.

When Cipolla's performance is advertised, this theme, essential to the first third of the story, reappears. The narrator says that, upon noticing the advertisement, his children "besieged" him to go to the show. He "had doubts." And he "gave way"—of course. Thus a bridge is built into the rest of the story where the narrator's dignified absence of energy is but one part of a more complex composition.

As he and his family walk to the hall for the performance, the narrator describes their path explicitly in terms of social class. Passing under the wall of the ruined palace, along a street with the "better shops" and then into a neighborhood of "poor fishing-huts," he proceeds "from the feudal, past the bourgeois into the proletarian." The hall, he says, was "among the proletariat." And, inside the hall, class distinctions persist. The bourgeoisie take their seats up front while the "fisherfolk"—later, the narrator calls them just "the populace"—stand. To this point, the story has tended to soft-pedal social divisions. It has stressed, instead, temperamental cleavages, associated with differences of nationality and geography. But now, abruptly, the social divisions are sharply emphasized as well.

As the audience waits for Cipolla to appear, the narrator extends his remarks on the topic. Referring to the sundry "fisherfolk"—"rough-and-ready youths with bare forearms crossed over their striped jerseys"—he says that he was "pleased" with the "colour and animation" they brought the occasion.

His children's reaction is notably different. They are "frankly delighted" to see the fisherfolk in the hall. For they know them. They have spoken Italian to them. They have helped pull in their nets. They actually have "friends among these people." Bridging the social gulf, the children point up its breadth; for their connection to "the populace" reveals, by contrast, the narrator's prissy disconnection.[17]

When, at last, Cipolla appears on stage, the narrator remarks on his weird appearance, comparing him to a bygone "charlatan and mountebank type." Is Cipolla, then, a unique figure, an alien? Or does he resonate with—taking to a ghastly, dramatic point—other figures and events and tendencies in the story? In the first take on the story, Cipolla is seen as enacting dangerous tendencies already revealed in the "ordinary humanity" of the town. What is noticed is his kinship not only to the crowd, but to officials of the Grand Hotel and the municipality as well. In the second take, a wholly different pattern of kinship comes to the fore. What now appears is Cipolla's affinity with the narrator himself.

Introducing Cipolla, the narrator notes his "self-satisfied air so characteristic of the deformed." Ask yourself: Which other figure in the story would you imagine as "self-satisfied"? Which "deformed"? Might it not be the narrator who comes to mind? In fact, evidence of the kinship between them mounts up right away. As Cipolla finishes with his first subject, the narrator reports on his "mock[ing]" tone to the young man—reminiscent of the narrator's own way of speaking about the local people. Like the narrator, Cipolla remarks on his "sensitiv[ity]" to insults and says he wishes to be treated "courteously" by the people. "I am a man who sets some store by himself," he says. He prides himself on the respect he has won "among the educated public," and from "brilliant and elevated audiences," another point of haughty affinity between the two of them. It is, he continues, "with my mental and spiritual parts that I conquer life—which after all only means conquering oneself." Here, yet again, he places himself alongside the narrator, in contrast to the unself-disciplined and sense-loving people of the town.[18]

As the show goes on, Cipolla's bond to the narrator becomes clearer. Cipolla takes "care not to molest the more select portion of his audience." Picking upon "two sturdy young louts," he remarks on "their heroic firmness of limb" in just the sort of ironic classical reference favored by the narrator. He is "elaborately patient and chivalrous" to fancy foreigners; but he shows only "derogatory" courtesy to the natives. Indeed, most of Cipolla's patter, patriotic and otherwise, is an extended, ironic put-down of the crowd. What he is doing, in effect, is giving a rambling version of the speech the narrator claims to have had on the tip of his tongue, but failed to deliver to the mob on the beach.

Behind this disdain is social distance and an assumption—Cipolla's, the narrator's—of social as well as "mental and spiritual" power over "the populace." At one point, echoing earlier remarks of the narrator, Cipolla says that a young man's big hands are "calculated" to do "service for the public." Returning the echo, the narrator notices a man he recognizes in the crowd who, he simply observes, "had served us several times, with neatness and dispatch."[19]

Cipolla, to be sure, likes to wield power. The narrator just likes to have it. Or, perhaps more precisely, Cipolla abuses power, whereas the narrator just wants to use it in a nearly invisible, taken-for-granted, manner. The difference is important. Still, the vital point here is that much of the sentiment driving

Cipolla in wielding power over the crowd is incipient in the narrator. Cipolla simply carries it to an extreme. Indeed, early in the evening, the narrator seems, briefly, to sense the affinity between them. He says that, as Cipolla brandished his whip, "involuntarily I made with my lips the sound that [the] whip had made when it cut the air."[20]

A while later, of course, the narrator starts to evolve a distaste for Cipolla. He describes his skill as "uncanny." He sees that it profanes the sort of rationality to which he is wedded. He begins to understand Cipolla as a challenge. Twice, one hotheaded young worker—the one who is dressed in the style of "the awakened Fatherland"—does step forward to resist, even rebel. Twice, Cipolla subdues, then humiliates him. But, remarkably, on neither of the two occasions does the narrator even muse about stepping forward with him. He recognizes the youth's "fighting spirit." But he thus only illuminates his own lack—even in imagination—of that spirit, even as Reason and Freedom are embattled. On the beach and at the Grand Hotel, the narrator considered resistance—and made a couple of dignified little gestures toward it. Here, however, there is nothing. How come?

That question arises alongside another. For, while the narrator is dormant, the crowd is passive as well. But with a difference. The narrator reports that "ill will" and *desire* to resist were rising among the crowd. He reports that "rebellion" was in the air. And he goes on to pose the issue: What was it that "kept such feelings in check"? The issue he doesn't raise is: Why was it that he did not share even these rebellious "feelings" of the crowd?

He speculates that what kept "rebellion from becoming overt" was not only Cipolla's skill as a hypnotist. It was also his "courtesy" and "stern self-confidence." How could courtesy and confidence overcome the rebelliousness of the crowd? Could the same qualities of bearing somehow have made the narrator even more completely passive? The answer has to do with social hierarchy, with the matter of social class introduced earlier. The working "populace" had been trained to submit to the self-confident demeanor of their "betters"; to stifle feelings of rebellion and solidarity with each other. Formal "derogatory" courtesy signaled authority that they were in the habit of obeying. The narrator sensed the same signals. But, from the other side of the social divide, he received a different message.

Cipolla's demeanor was by habit his own. It was, quite plausibly, out of the question for him even to "feel" rebellion against the representation of himself. The "populace" is something from which he had defined himself as distant, superior. He could not begin to join the "ordinary people"—including the noisy, unrefined young man with his "heart at the end of his tongue"—in any kind of active solidarity, in any kind of common cause.[21]

A bit later, a young gentleman, an Italian, rises to resist Cipolla and "assert his own will." Although the narrator admires his "proud, finely chiselled features," even now he does not join the resistance. Calling the young man an "apostle of freedom," he shows that his own isolation is rooted not only in estrangement from "ordinary people"—and from southerners in general—but also in his very idea of "freedom." The narrator lauds this man because he stands *alone* to assert, very coolly, his *autonomy* as an individual. But Cipolla subdues him as he had the workingman. He says: "Freedom exists, and also the will exists; but freedom of the will does not exist, for a will that aims [only] at its own freedom aims at the unknown." In this strangely abstract formulation—which thus demands attention—Cipolla is flatly stating an important insight. The capacity—

the energy—to assert and resist power can only decay in the absence of some concrete purpose rooted in a concrete connection to other people. In the absence, that is, of *political* purpose and connection, it cannot flourish. And it is precisely this sort of failure of *political* energy that characterizes the humiliation, by Cipolla, of the crowd—and, to a much greater degree, of the narrator as well.[22]

The one person in the whole story who does try to act politically in opposition to Cipolla is the patriotic workingman who is twice subjugated. On the second occasion, he gives a very minimal example of political energy, defying Cipolla:

> "That will do," said he loudly. "That's enough jokes about Torre. We all come from the place and we won't stand strangers making fun of it. These two chaps are our friends. Maybe they are no scholars, but even so they may be straighter than some folks in the room who are so free with their boasts about Rome, though they did not build it either."[23]

What defeats him is that the "we" he invokes does not emerge to back him up. The others do not seem to share his energy. They have been trained out of it. And political energy that isn't shared is, necessarily, destined to frustration.

Now, there is an intermission in the show. On the second take, this is an important part of the story. For, here, the narrator begins to focus on the problem. "You are sure to ask," he asserts, "why we did not choose . . . to go." He complains that Cipolla "paralysed our resolve." However, he is aware that answer will not do. For this question is tied to the question of why he didn't leave town earlier. "[T]he two questions," he sees, "are one and the same." And what is the answer? "[Y]ou may call it inertia," he shrugs. He is inching toward the truth here. He now recognizes that it is not energy, but the absence of energy that is the problem. But energy to do what? To leave? What he still doesn't get is that what is lacking—the lack at the core of the story—is the energy to act, act politically. Political energy, of course, involves getting into a struggle. That he cannot do.[24]

As the performance resumes, he takes one more step—his last, small step—toward insight. Identifying with the crowd at least in its passivity, he states, "we all cowered" before Cipolla. Describing a "well-built, soldierly man . . . unable to lift his arm" under the hypnotic influence, he seems to empathize with the "stately" man. And when Cipolla humiliates the landlord of the pensione where he is staying, he sympathizes openly: "Poor Signor Angiolieri, so quiet, so bald!" Now that Cipolla is picking on more elevated members of the audience, the narrator can feel some real connection. His sympathy, in turn, spurs his insight. Signor Angiolieri "did not look," he observes, "as though he would know how to defend his happiness, even against powers much less" potent. Is he reflecting, here, on his own impotence? And, finally, when the Italian gentleman vows, again, to resist and fails, the narrator offers a diagnosis that echoes Cipolla's earlier abstract pronouncement and suggests that he has learned something:

> If I understand what was going on, it was the negative character of the young man's fighting position which was his undoing. It is likely that *not* willing is not a practicable state of mind; *not* to want to do something may be in the long run a mental content impossible to subsist on. Between not willing a certain thing and not willing at all—in other words, yielding to another person's will—there may lie too small a space for the idea of freedom to squeeze into.

He sees now that freedom requires some *positive* purpose, but he does not—to the end—recognize that it requires some *collective* engagement and mobilization of energy as well.[25]

The last two tableaux of the show teach this unlearned lesson. The first is the "dissolute" group set to dancing on the stage. With the group is the gentleman whose assertion of individual pride, the narrator vainly supposes, might have been a "rallying-point." It is, in fact, Cipolla who is engaging and "rallying" the people. What he achieves—in superficial, debased, perverse form—is a collective mobilization of energy. And what is remarkable is that the dancers appear to be happy. In fact, the noble gentleman is "having a better time than . . . in his hour of pride." They have let themselves go. What they have thrown off is not so much "the burden of voluntary choice," as the narrator theorizes. After all, they may never have experienced voluntary choice. The burden they have been relieved of— even if artificially and just for a moment—is that of day-to-day isolation and impotence. Though the nectar is not real, they can taste in imagination the freedom that has been squeezed out of them.

The final tableau places Mario beside Cipolla on the platform. When Cipolla summoned him, "Mario obeyed." "[I]t was only too easy," the narrator observes, "to see why he obeyed. After all, obedience was his calling in life." When, early in the evening, Cipolla had hypnotized his first subject, he had talked of "divid[ing] up the willing and the doing" and called it a "[d]ivision of labour." Now, at the end of the evening, the connection between the division of labor and hypnosis is once again made clear.

This connection is manifest not only in Mario's obedience; it shows up also in the narrator's reflections on Mario. He says that he has seen the young man "nearly every day." Yet he says, "We knew him humanly without knowing him personally if I may make that distinction." How so? He knows what the young man looks like; he can describe his "dreamy" behavior; he reports that Mario's father is a petty clerk and that his mother takes in washing. But, though he has observed Mario, he hasn't engaged him. Why? Inadvertently, he provides the answer. Mario's "white waiter's-coat," states the narrator, "became him better than the . . . suit he wore." He describes Mario's hands as "slender and delicate." "They were hands," the narrator blithers on, "by which one liked being served." (He is once again echoing one of Cipolla's earlier remarks.) If Mario obeys because he is a waiter, the narrator remains a passive—a hypnotized—watcher of Mario's down-fall for much the same reason.[26]

Once Mario is on the stage, Cipolla launches an interrogation. He begins with his usual formal courtesy, congratulating Mario on his "classic name" and his work as a "cup-bearer, a Ganymede." "I like that," he asserts, "it is [a] classical allusion." (Thus, he echoes back to the narrator one last time.) With the preliminaries over, Cipolla turns from Mario's work life to his personal life. "[H]ave you troubles?" he asks. Mario promptly denies it. Cipolla, all solici-tude, continues: "You *have* troubles . . . [I]t is a girl, isn't it? You have love troubles?" After someone in the crowd supplies the girl's name, Cipolla shifts into high gear:

> "But Silvestra, your Silvestra—ah, what a girl that is! . . . Brings your heart into your mouth to see her walk or laugh or breathe, she is so lovely. . . . And she makes you suffer, this angel," went on Cippola. . . . "I know what you are thinking: what does this Cipolla, with his little physical defect, know about love? Wrong, all wrong, he knows a lot."

On the first take, this is a glaring invasion of privacy. But on double take, it is more poignant than that.

After all, it is the sole time in the story when an adult even pretends to reach out to someone "personally" across social barriers. It represents—again, in a debased form—the possibility of connection. That it *is* debased—that Cipolla is making fun of Mario, manipulating him, ultimately hypnotizing Mario to kiss him as Silvestra—evokes a powerful sense of absence. The capacity of the children to connect "personally" to "the populace" stands as a contrast to the adult incapacity. But Cipolla's mockery and manipulation is not just a contrast—it is the twisting of the knife that makes it impossible not to see—and, more, to feel—what is missing.

Of course, rebellion has been missing, too. Now, Mario rebels. He shoots Cipolla. Why? And why Mario? To be sure, he has been humiliated more completely—and he appears to be more "melancholy"—than the others. Is that all there is to it? The narrator makes a point of depicting Mario at the moment before he goes up on stage. He portrays the young man as "thickset" with "heavy lidded eyes," "thick lips," and a "low forehead." "[T]he whole upper half of his face," he observes, "retreated behind the lower." Hardly the image of a romantic Individualist hero. Rather, it is a primitive image. Indeed, the narrator notes Mario's "primitive" mien.

And, as it happens, his primitivity draws important elements of the story to a political point. From what source, in the end, is the energy required for freedom going to come? From the elevated, refined, "civilized" stratum of personality or society, that of the narrator? Or from a more primitive stratum, that of Mario?

But is the end of the story "a liberation" as the narrator supposes it to be? The individual who stood up to Cipolla has been disarmed and awaits the arriving police. The crowd is in chaos. The narrator leaves, along with his family. This is no liberation. What's most striking is what does not happen. The crowd doesn't rally around Mario. The crowd doesn't rebel. The narrator doesn't learn what he needs to learn: that freedom requires political mobilization of "ordinary people" and that, for purposes of politics, you should embrace your lot as one "ordinary" person among many, taking to heart the fear and hope that is the lot of us all.[27]

That is the second take on the story.

Pause here for a moment. If you have read *Mario and the Magician,* ask yourself which of the takes on it best matches your own—or best matches your

initial reaction to it. If you haven't read it, ask yourself which telling of the story evokes the deepest
response, which one resonates most powerfully for
you. And ask, then, which is most likely to resonate
powerfully for the people you know, evoking the
deepest response in our contemporary culture of
politics and law, in our imagination of constitutionalism.

= II =

V

"HIGHER" LAW?

V

I WANT NOW to turn to the sensibility that animates and structures today's conventional discourse about constitutional law. This sensibility (so I have claimed) is made up of assumptions about, images of, and attitudes toward ordinary people as active and energetic participants, singly and collectively, in politics and government. It implicates a chain of reactions to the imagined reality and possibility of democracy. What is "contained" in reaction to *Mario and the Magician* spreads through every cell of routine argument over the meaning and application of the Constitution.

My approach here, more didactic than before, will be both diagnostic and hortatory. Identifying two very general takes on ordinary political energy—parallelling the two already sketched—I'll assert that one is dominant in constitutional law discourse. I'll go on to diagnose and evaluate the effects and bases of its dominance. Then, I'll urge a reversal of attitude. I'll urge consideration of the other, subordinated take on democracy, pointing to certain ways it might affect our discourse. I'll suggest that what are at stake, in the end, are conventional notions not only about the mission of constitutional law, but also about its status as "higher" than ordinary law born of ordinary politics.

Addressing so broad a topic in so abbreviated a compass means I'll be painting with a broad brush. Probably more precisely, I'll be using a paint roller—maybe even a spray can. Let me stress again: I am not out to prove or demonstrate anything. What I *am* out to do is provoke you, jar you to see familiar general issues of constitutional law in an unconventional way, to try out another take on them. For that purpose, all I'm offering—all I need to offer—is my own take on the conventions of the current discourse and on an alternative, one that is significantly different.

Two "Takes" on Ordinary Political Energy

Put very simply, the two ways of imagining the political energy of ordinary people are as follows:

One imagines it to be a problem; the other imagines its absence as the problem. One presumes political peace to be a good. The other worries that peace is but a mark of popular passivity, presumed to be bad. For one, the active political involvement of ordinary people not only threatens the peace, but tends to debase the quality of government and even risk oppression as well. For the other, it is not only fundamental to the quality of government, but also the most essential inoculation against oppression.

That, however, puts the difference *too* simply. I'll stretch out my characterization, elaborating on certain elements and pointing to certain bases of the two takes on ordinary political energy—but with one important proviso. The proviso is that I am referring neither to "reasons" for, nor "empirical support" for "beliefs" about the world. What I am talking about is assumptions, images, and attitudes. Taken together, they don't make up a theory: I'm not interested here in political, moral, or legal theory. I am interested in portraying nothing more—or less—than a sensibility.

It is a sensibility, as I've said, that is "about" what ordinary people are like when energized to act, singly or collectively, in politics and government. I ought to clarify that at this point: It is also about what people *in general* are like when moved by what is "ordinary" in them—as distinct from what is "higher" or more "refined"—to act politically. That is to say, it is about what people in general are like when they act *like* ordinary people. At the heart of this sensibility is a distinction between different sorts of people as potential actors in politics—but, more fundamentally, it is between different sorts of attributes.

For the sake of convenience, I'll refer now to the two takes on ordinary political energy in crude shorthand. The first one I'll denominate the Anti-Populist sensibility. I'll call the second, by contrast, the Populist sensibility. The purport of this shorthand, beyond mere convenience, will slowly unfold as I diagnose and evaluate the two of them.

To the Anti-Populist sensibility, ordinary political energy—and, hence, a politics animated by it—is problematic because of attributes that set it apart from, and identify it as qualitatively inferior to, more "refined" sources of political participation. To start with, ordinary energy is imagined as springing from, as well as activating, states of mind and temperament presumed to be defective:

emotional	as opposed to	reasonable
ignorant	as opposed to	informed
fuzzy-minded	as opposed to	clear-headed
simple-minded	as opposed to	complex

These defective states of mind are, in turn, associated with a tendency to irresponsibility:

short-sighted	as opposed to	far-sighted
narrow-minded	as opposed to	broad-minded
self-centered	as opposed to	public-spirited
fickle	as opposed to	steadfast
arbitrary	as opposed to	principled
low standards	as opposed to	high standards

Unfortunately, they go relatively unfiltered and unchecked:

impulsive	as opposed to	deliberate
peremptory	as opposed to	dialogic
closed-minded	as opposed to	open-minded

What is worse, these states of mind tend to be vulnerable to influence and manipulation:

conformist	as opposed to	independent
suggestible	as opposed to	critical

And, what is even worse, this vulnerability to influence and manipulation is fed by a volatile insecurity:

anxious	as opposed to	composed
resentful	as opposed to	magnanimous
angry	as opposed to	placable

When political *energy* activates attributes so defective, the resultant behavior tends, then, to be defective:

hot	as opposed to	cool
rude	as opposed to	considerate
vulgar	as opposed to	civilized
reckless	as opposed to	prudent
intoxicated	as opposed to	sober
invasive	as opposed to	restrained
abusive	as opposed to	respectful
moralistic	as opposed to	tolerant
prejudiced	as opposed to	fair
tribal	as opposed to	cosmopolitan
mob-like	as opposed to	statesmanlike

Ordinary political energy is imagined to be problematic in two related respects: It makes for a politics that is not just low in quality, but dangerous as well.

Its low quality and dangerousness are most dramatically (and conventionally) imagined in the collective behavior of ordinary people acting as "crowds." Think of the crowd on the beach in Thomas Mann's story—agitated, moralistic, tribal—bullying the narrator and his family. Or think of the herd-like crowd "led" by Cipolla, applauding his mixture of abuse and patriotic sentiment. Bullied itself, it cheers the bully. Yet the defects of ordinary political energy are not imagined as being limited to such collective behavior. On the contrary, they are seen as tending also to infect the action of individuals, particularly those responding to or currying favor from groups of people. Think of the town official who extracts "ransom" from Mann's narrator,[28] or think of Cipolla himself. Even individuals exercising power independently—exposed to no direct group influence—are hardly immune to the virus. Think of the agitated client of the Grand Hotel, fearing "acoustic" infection by a child's cough, who insists that the narrator and his family move out of their room.[29] Or think of the official of the hotel who complies, arbitrarily favoring certain clients, for the second time, over others.

In a world imagined as charged with ordinary political energy of this sort, the Anti-Populist response is to pursue one of two main courses. The first is withdrawal: celebration and cultivation of privacy and of peace, seeking space insulated from infection by politics. The narrator of *Mario and the Magician* chooses this course. The second is transcendence: insulation of a more "refined," higher-minded mode of political participation in an exalted realm, a realm from which, then, to try to contain or to retard, to tame or to manipulate, the forces of ordinary politics. What unites the two is not just worry about the danger of such politics, but also insistence on eschewing intimate involvement in it. Behind the insistence on insulation is fear, to be sure, but (at least a genteel) loathing as well. At the wellspring of the Anti-Populist sensibility is disdain—a "looking down" on the political energy of ordinary people as well as on the "lower" elements of oneself drawn out by energetic political exertion and engagement on a level with ordinary people.

What, now, is the Populist sensibility like? It might bathe, I suppose, in the "romance of the ordinary," flipping upside-down the Anti-Populist identification of who is refined and who is vulgar. That is, it might involve a notion that it is ordinary people who tend to be reasonable, public-spirited, and respectful—and elites that tend to be emotional, self-centered, abusive, and so on down the list of contrasting positive and negative qualities. No doubt, such a romantic populism has had (and still has) some currency in American culture. (Think of the famous Frank Capra movies.) But there are three problems with it. First, it just is not very plausible— especially at this moment in history—to take so high-falutin a view of the ordinary, the baseline, in human nature.[30] Second, to do so isn't even interesting. For, third, the fundamental issue posed by the Anti-Populist sensibility has to do with the idea that *some* people are fit for active participation in political life and that *some* are not. It has to do, that is, with the hierarchy of *qualities* by which one is distinguished from the other. So, as a deep contrast to the Anti-Populist sensibility, what we need is a very different take on any such hierarchy of qualities.

This might involve, once again, a flipping upside-down of the Anti-Populist sensibility. The qualities Anti-Populism imagines to be inferior might be envisioned as superior. And vice versa. Thus emotion might be celebrated as superior to reason. And so on. Once again, this sort of counter-culture populism has had and has some currency. But it runs up against a similar problem of plausibility, and it similarly evades the basic issue presented by Anti-Populism: the particular way it bisects general qualities as suited or unsuited to political participation. For a deep contrast to the Anti-Populist sensibility, we need a take on political energy that is oriented in terms of different coordinates.

At the heart of the Populist sensibility is a refusal to look at political energy in terms of superior and inferior qualities imagined along these Anti-Populist lines. In the place of those coordinates, it substitutes two others that are intimately related to one another. Taken together, they produce a real shift, a reorientation of sensibility.

On one axis, the Populist sensibility measures *how much* ordinary political energy is being expressed— how widespread is its expression, to what extent are individuals engaging one another politically— assuming that expression of such energy is better than passivity or insulation. This means energetic activity in politics *by* ordinary people, and it means engagement *with* ordinary people, on a common level. This sort of activity is imagined as superior not because it is somehow elevated or refined, but for simpler reasons. It makes for better government— responsive to ordinary people whom it purports to serve, its purported sovereign. What is more, it's a tonic. That is, it is good for the *vitality* of all who take part in it, collectively as well as singly.

Passivity and/or insulation, by contrast, are imagined as unhealthy in the case both of individuals (think of Mann's narrator) and of groups (Cipolla's audience). The assumption is that such self-confinement is nurtured by, and nurtures, states of mind and temperament that are defective:

meek	as opposed to	courageous
paralyzed	as opposed to	vigorous
role-bound	as opposed to	spontaneous
isolated	as opposed to	connected

These attributes are imagined as based in—and enforced by—repression, whether psychological repression of ordinary, self-assertive instincts or social repression of vitality by role-expectations, mandated explicitly or implicitly:

inhibited	as opposed to	expansive
other-directed	as opposed to	inner-directed
diffident	as opposed to	self-confident

These kinds of repression are imagined, in turn, as inviting as well as fostering another kind of repression, a political repression of the weak by the strong:

submissive	as opposed to	vigilant
conformist	as opposed to	independent
suggestible	as opposed to	critical

Thus, political passivity and/or insulation don't just erode political liberty—they actually pose a threat to it.

Of course, inhibition is a sort of refinement. Release of inhibition may well involve release of "ordinary" emotions such as anger or self-righteousness, which are crude and even aggressive. To a Populist sensibility, such emotions aren't the whole sum and substance of ordinary energy. But, to the extent they *are* part and parcel of an expression of ordinary political energy, they do not render it worthy of disdain.

It is exactly such disdain that is measured on the second axis of the Populist sensibility. Disdain for the political energy of ordinary people—and for the sorts of "ordinary" attributes supposedly brought out by political engagement with them—is envisioned as deeply problematic. It is a defective attitude since it involves cutting oneself off from possibilities of political assertion and engagement and fosters passive withdrawal. What is worse, it can—if disseminated widely and solidified in institutions affecting everyday life—erode self-confidence among ordinary people and metastasize political passivity. And, worse yet, it may embolden elites to claim transcendence, securing an elevated position from which to try to contain, control, or manipulate ordinary political energy. Think of Cipolla, with his toxic superiority complex, manipulating his audience. Think, too, of the narrator—Cipolla's prim double—whose disdainful insulation takes shape as pathetic passivity, but who senses an affinity to and for the active, transcendent power of the "magician."

What is striking here is the relation of the two takes on ordinary political energy. To a Populist sensibility, the nemesis is represented by the Anti-Populist sensibility. And vice versa. The two aren't just distinct; they aren't just opposites; they are at each other's throats. Both of them resonate for most of us, I believe. Yet they struggle for predominance in our minds and in our hearts.

The Predominance of Anti-Populism

In the minds and hearts of most American constitutional lawyers, an Anti-Populist sensibility appears to predominate now. Is this statement surprising? If it is, how can I back it up? If it isn't, no backup may be needed. But to the extent that the predominance of the Anti-Populist take on ordinary political energy is dismissed as obvious, its effects on the conventional discourse of constitutional law may well pass without notice. What, then, are they?

The effects, I believe, involve an inflation of constitutional law, its grandiose puffing as law imagined to be "higher"—*because "better"*—than ordinary law made by ordinary people. Like one who ingests sour milk and who, as a consequence, inflates, we constitutional lawyers have fed on disdain for the political energy of ordinary people. So, we have bloated not just our image of ourselves, but also of the law we aspire to serve, making it, in cultural effect, a vast bubble of heated gas floating above ordinary experience—or what is worse, a weight, politically condescending and repressive, frequently humiliating, even suffocating.[31]

To back up—if not support or, still less, establish—the diagnosis, I'll illustrate it a little bit. I'll pick and sketch quickly a few illustrations from a fund of material that serves my purpose for two reasons. It is a fund of symptoms of the sensibility predominant in discourse about constitutional law. And it is immediately accessible, without research, to constitutional lawyers, who can check what I have to say, thinking of other, perhaps inconsistent, illustrations. The fund I'll draw upon is the fund of banal statements, or clichés, at the tips of the tongues of all of us who know how to practice constitutional argument. Should it seem too low-life to mention nothing but clichés of everyday argument, I'll offer also, for good measure, an illustration or two from the world of high society—the world, that is, of constitutional theory as practiced in law schools.[32]

Let's start with a master cliché: the notion that majoritarianism or majority rule is the background, the norm against which constitutional law proceeds. We talk of deferring to the majority as presumptively necessary. The counter-majoritarian character of judicial review thus is described as a "difficulty." Doesn't this majoritarian rhetoric undercut my diagnosis? Doesn't it suggest that the predominant sensibility of our discourse is really Populist? That it is a celebration of ordinary political energy? In a word: No, it doesn't.

When we say we "defer" to "the majority," we tend in so doing to express an attitude toward the majority. Attitudes typically expressed are of three kinds, and all of them are relatively disdainful of ordinary political energy. Deference is sometimes presented, first of all, as a sort of refined withdrawal. Getting out of the way of a big, vulgar group, declining to engage with it: the "deference" conveyed is haughty and ironic, perhaps respectful of brute force, or strictly formal authority, but that's all. (Think of Mann's narrator.) In this vein, we hold our noses and claim we are deferring to the (implicitly irrational) "preferences" of the majority. At other times, we take what would seem to be the opposite tack. We claim we are deferring to the "wisdom" or "judgment" or "experience" of the majority. Here, the irony is thicker, heavier. (Think of the "derogatory courtesy" of Cipolla.) We use these terms in pro forma fashion. What is more, we use such flattery simply to justify deference—to say we don't care to look behind it, to inquire whether it's deserved. This sort of formal, *explicitly empty* flattery is—at least in part—an expression of courtly disdain.

Even more scornful, finally, is the routine assertion that the majority does "rule." The actual truth of this description is rarely questioned in the conventional discourse. Rarely is it noticed as *open* to question.[33] Yet even as we repeat the assertion, we know that the majority of citizens usually does not vote; we know something about special interest groups, lobbyists, and the rest. Granted, a silent majority may be silent because it is satisfied. And, granted, the chance that the silence might end one day may exert indirect influence. But the fact remains that routine talk of rule not just by a majority of legislators, but by "the majority"—as if it were a fact—is striking. What should we make of a man who keeps repeating that because women are a majority, therefore they "rule" (at least indirectly)? (Think of Cipolla insisting he is the servant of the crowd.) What attitude, if not disdain, is conveyed by this routine?

If ironic praise of "majority rule" is the background noise of typical constitutional discourse, in the foreground is a very different theme: explicit and elaborate criticism—criticism not just of the "system" of majority rule, but also of the majority itself, of ordinary people who are in the majority. Indeed, the animating *mission* of modern constitutional law is conventionally described as the correction of failures allegedly endemic to majority rule. The mission is to safeguard "The Individual" or "minorities" or even some governmental bodies (the states, the executive, the judiciary, the legislature) supposedly threatened by the force of ordinary political energy. The threat is portrayed as due in part—

but only a secondary part—to defects in the institutions through which that force is employed. More basically, the threat is envisioned as coming from the base and dangerous quality of the political energy driving alike the majority and the ordinary people who hold official power in its name.

Thus, by rote, we construct our "activist" constitutional arguments with derogatory depictions, whether explicit or implicit, of ordinary political energy. We talk of prejudice or self-aggrandizement, oppressiveness or impulsiveness, short-sightedness or simple-mindedness, as innate propensities. In the modern era as in the *Lochner* era, we pick these descriptions of ordinary *political* actors from the Anti-Populist candy box, satisfying the sweet tooth that we, as *legal* actors, take for granted. And so, filling up on insults, we become more and more full of ourselves.[34]

The pervasive Anti-Populist sensibility is also expressed in the scope of the rights that typically are set up against the depredation of ordinary political energy. For, even as this sensibility calls rights forth, it obstructs their growth. If there is one almost unchallenged cliché in our talk about rights nowadays, it is that, whatever a constitutional right may be, it may not be "absolute." How come? The assumption is that an absolute right would be "abused." And why? It would be abused, we assume, because the exercise of rights is animated by the same sort of ordinary political energy—with all its defects—that the rights are meant to protect against in the first place. Thus to check and moderate, and so to "improve," the exercise both of rights and government, we must, we say, keep both in gently held leading strings of a "reasonable"—therefore "higher"—constitutional law.

When we justify the authority of judges to pursue the imagined mission of constitutional law—and, in the process, to overturn decisions by political actors—we talk in terms of the supposedly *superior quality* of judicial decisionmaking. And, again, those terms typically are drawn from the Anti-Populist lexicon. Whether because of training or acculturation, tenure in office or a shaping of issues by the judicial process, judges, we say, are insulated from the pressures of ordinary politics. They can transcend ordinary politics. By dint of their quality of mind and temperament, they can oppose it diametrically. When political actors are emotional, they can be reasonable; when political actors are self-regarding, they can be public-spirited. They can speak the "sober second thought." They can represent our "better" selves. Because judges can be so very superior to political actors, they are well suited, we profess, to contain or tame the lowly, threatening tendency of ordinary political energy through interpretation and application of the Constitution.

Yet lurking even within judges we see the stirring of ordinary political energy. We worry that it may distort their "reading" of constitutional law. Thus we fuss over the extent to which their work is infected by "personal values" or "political commitments." And we insist that they be insulated not only from ordinary politics, but from these baser aspects of themselves, that they transcend and contain or tame them. We differ among ourselves as to how—and to what degree—this sort of insulation and transcendence may be accomplished.[35] In the last few decades, our differences have led us to become more conscious and much more demanding of abstract "methodologies" of reasoning on constitutional topics. As a result, the general standards to which we hold this "reasoning" have undergone swift and steady inflation.

The inflation of standards has, in turn, led to a displacement of status in the conventional discourse of constitutional law. On one hand, it has eroded the capacity of ordinary people to take part in—and even understand—such argument. Citizens, including political actors charged with a responsibility to consider constitutional law, become its spectators, fascinated mainly by their distance from it. Even judges, ordinary people wearing robes, find it more and more difficult to draft opinions that go out in their names. On the other hand, the escalation of standards has amplified the voice of legal academia. Law clerks, recent graduates at the top of their class at top law schools, draft more and more judicial opinions. Judges employ more and more clerks. Professors criticize the opinions. New students learn to write "better" opinions than the ones drafted by their predecessors. The conventional discourse of constitutional law breathes in the warm air of the academy, rises over the heads of many to whom it is supposedly addressed, and then sends down a subtle message of inadequacy to everyone who is not "in the know."[36]

Since the 1980s, the special contribution of academia to constitutional law has involved something called "constitutional theory." A potentially interesting venture, constitutional theory promised to merge the inflated talk about "methodologies" of "reasoning" into more open-textured, openly controversial talk about competing visions of the good political life that somehow might inform constitutional argument.[37] To date, this theory has not had much impact on the practice of the law. In fact, it has been mainly confined to a small lapful of professors. Its career is instructive, however, for the way it has bent to the manifest magnetism of the Anti-Populist sensibility.

At the core of recent constitutional theory is the idea of "community."[38] In particular, we have talked of a "republican"—as opposed to a "liberal"—vision of our political life. The focus has been on the importance of the "common interest" and of "civic virtue," understood as commitment to seeking the "common interest" through political engagement. In the 1970s, when I first organized my own constitutional law class in these terms, I treated the competing visions simply as images, rhetorical motifs informing and enabling conflict within the law. And I viewed the republican vision itself as conflicted: One might imagine "civic virtue" in terms of energetic, uninhibited political participation by anyone and everyone, seeing the inclusiveness and energy of politics as the best guarantor of the common good. (That is to say, a Populist spin on the "republican" vision.) Or, on the other hand, one might imagine "civic virtue" in terms of "reason," a process of wise "deliberation" over the "common interest," transcending the defects of ordinary politics. (That is, an Anti-Populist spin.) I understood this conflict internal to the republican vision to open in the law more room for the clash of ideas. However, the constitutional theory of the last decade has developed in a very different direction. It has revolved about the Anti-Populist version of republican community, scorning, wiping out, the Populist version.[39] In lofty new stagings of old salutes to "reasoned deliberation"—honoring it again as being better and so "higher" than ordinary political energy—it has costumed conventional disdain for ordinary energy in a powdered wig. In fact, the disdain has been so powerful as to push a lot of constitutional theory to transform the republican vision into "republican*ism*"—a principle or doctrine, supposedly based authoritatively in the world of the framers, that should be "applied" to decide constitutional cases. Thus it has responded to the old urge to cook up another methodology of decisionmaking, claiming again to transcend all that is "ordinary" in decisionmakers, again to close down rather than open up ideological dispute. At the end of a decade, what this pompous theory has done is simply incubate a further inflation of the discourse.[40]

In truth, the high rate of inflation of the discourse—driven by disdain for ordinary political energy—is not confined to the law schools or the courtrooms. It tends to show itself wherever and whenever we talk about the Constitution. The pomposity, the grandiosity, the pretense of "higher" law: all are taken for granted. We appear not fully to grasp how this inflated discourse *de*flates ordinary people as political actors. That, too, we take for granted.

Let me give a couple examples. Think, first, of any discussion you've heard about proposals to call a new constitutional convention. Think of how skepticism about it is expressed. Wouldn't a convention be filled with ordinary politicians? How could one of *them* possibly sit where James Madison sat? Isn't it probable such a convention would "get out of hand"? Wouldn't it respond to popular opinion, cater to immediate desires, make a big mess? Isn't it frightening that ordinary people say they don't "believe in" The Bill of Rights? Could we let *them* meddle with The Constitution?

Or consider this anecdote. For a few days, over New Year's Eve, an invited group of fancy profes-

sionals—"influential, well-connected, very success-
ful people," we are told—get together at a resort in
South Carolina for a "Renaissance Weekend" to talk
with one another. The Weekend is famous because
the President has long been a participant. At the last
annual convocation, one participant—Dean of a Di-
vinity School and described as a "believer in Renaissance"—mentioned the original constitutional convention in order to shed light on what he and his
friends are up to:

> "I think the fundamental vision of democracy is
> that politics is a matter of rational persuasion,"
> said Ronald Thiemann, dean of the Harvard Di-
> vinity School. "That was clearly the view of the
> best [get that?] of the Federalists. They also un-
> derstood, of course, that force was sometimes nec-
> essary, but they knew that any force had to rest
> on a base of rational discussion, the sort of thing
> that is cultured in settings like this one."[41]

Think about it.

Why Do a "Double Take"?

All right, you say, it's obvious enough that the Anti-
Populist sensibility is predominant in contemporary

constitutional law. Quite probably its effect is to inflate conventional discourse about the law. And maybe it produces discourse that is rather insensitive, even condescending, to our ordinary experience—maybe even repressive of ordinary energy. But so what? What's really wrong with that? Isn't that what constitutional law has always been like? Isn't it what the framers meant it to be like? Why even try to think about what difference an enhanced Populist sensibility might make in the discourse of constitutional law? Why even begin to question the image of constitutional law as "higher" law? Why try to "do a double take" on ordinary political energy?

I'll answer these questions by sketching three arguments. In a way, they are three counterarguments. For they take hold of, and then attempt to turn upside down, what I think are three principal sources of the conventional unwillingness to imagine ordinary political energy—and so constitutional law—in a different pattern. Each of these sources is located in the realm of sensibility. Hence, once again, I'll draw on our common fund of clichés to illustrate what I have to say about this resistance to re-imagination.

The first of these sources of resistance is a chronic fetishism of the Constitution, constitutional law, and the Supreme Court. Such fetishism—extravagant if not obsessive reverence for the icons, liturgies, and orthodoxies of Our Constitutionalism to which quasi-supernatural powers, beyond ordinary human agency, are commonly attributed—has waxed and waned over the decades. But over the last several decades, in the face of a variety of fundamental challenges, it has proved remarkably persistent and surprisingly potent.

To an extent, of course, this fetishism is just a symptom of the predominant Anti-Populist sensibility, just one more aspect of the inflation it sparks in discourse about the Constitution. At the same time, however, it has a special feedback effect. For, once established, it works to "lock in" the Anti-Populist imagination of ordinary politics and of "higher" law that gave it birth in the first place.

Contemporary constitutional fetishism takes two primary forms. The first involves an imagination of the Constitution not as amenable to a variety of interpretations—each plausible according to its own assumptions—but as having one "correct" meaning, founded in a body of "correct" assumptions. Portrayed as having one meaning, it can then be portrayed as having a determinate life *of its own*—an *object* inspiring obedience or maybe even faith. When evoked to sanctify the predominant sensibility, this image enhances its appeal. Invoked to resist efforts to contest—or claim the contestibility of—the predominant sensibility, it entrenches this sensibility. In this vein, we pontificate that the framers or long tradition—or whatever—planted Anti-Populist assumptions "in" constitutional law which now, on its own, mandates these assumptions. More generally and subliminally, this fetishism helps "lock in" the Anti-Populist sensibility by suggesting that constitutional law is "higher" not simply in a qualitative, but in an idolatrous, sense of the word.[42]

The other conspicuous sort of contemporary constitutional fetishism is precisely attuned to enhance the assumed qualitative superiority of constitutional law. What it involves is imagination of our Constitution not simply as terribly valuable, but terribly vital and vulnerable as well—so vital and so vulnerable that any meddling with it, any infection of it by ordinary politics, could lead to absolute disaster. Thus we talk of one or another "delicate" balance embodied in it. We depict it as "fragile"—intending that as ultimate praise. Testifying against a proposed amendment requiring a balanced federal budget, an expert said it would "cheapen" what he named "the most precious legacy we have to leave to our children, the Constitution." He warned, it was reported, that "the disrespect that now goes to politicians" might well "spread to the Constitution itself."[43] Along the same lines, we describe political situations—particularly those involving the extension or abuse of executive power—in hyperbolic terms as "constitutional crises." Iran-Contra or Watergate or the Pentagon Papers: each of them supposedly shows how vital and vulnerable is our Constitution, how thin the membrane of law, how threatening to it the coarse energy released by ordinary politics.[44] The support such sentiment gives the predominant Anti-Populist sensibility is obvious.

These two sorts of fetishism—voiced with differing intensity, as well as in differing proportions, by conservatives and liberals—are now taken for granted. If for a moment we stop and think about them, however, they may deflate with a pop. For we all, liberals and conservatives, have clearly in the backs of our minds lessons taught by the legal realists. We recall the realist critique of egregious constitutional fetishism in the *Lochner* era.[45] We even cite that critique against one another. When we indulge our own, no-less-egregious fetishism, we do it in manifest bad faith. Appreciating that, we should reject it. In rejecting it, we start to unravel the costume of the Anti-Populist outlook—freeing ourselves of this least deeply-rooted of the sources of resistance to re-imagination of Anti-Populist assumptions.

The second source of resistance goes a lot deeper. It is not just a symptom specific to constitutional discourse. Rather, it is rooted in the political and social context of that discourse. So, it cannot be deflated simply by pointing to contradictions within conventional talk about constitutional law. Yet—because it involves aspects of a usually taken-for-granted sensibility—appreciation of its implications may help free us from the blinders it imposes.

The disdain for ordinary political energy at work in constitutional law is not at all peculiar to it. To the contrary, this disdain is embedded in the sensibility of "the well-educated class." Members of this class fancy that they are properly "the governing class"—that it is people like them who should hold important positions in government. Yet government tends to involve, even depend upon, politics. That, in turn, makes "the well-educated class" anxious. For there is no denying that politics is going to involve—and may involve close contact with—other sorts of people. In politics, ordinary people may even get the upper hand. This specter tends to evoke, in one shape or another, the sort of disdain for ordinary political energy that finds a voice, an especially eloquent voice, in constitutional discourse.[46]

This is a very old story, to be sure. The tendency of a self-imagined "governing class" to fear and to loathe the rise of political challengers is familiar. Often, challenged social and economic elites have infused their own disdainful sensibility into the law. What is somewhat newer is the special insecurity of today's elite. Identifying the top dogs of his own period, Professor Felix Frankfurter "had time and patience only for the brilliant and the boys of old and wealthy families."[47] Nowadays, who knows which are "old and wealthy families"? Who cares? The very phrase has lost its resonance. Today, "the brilliant" are on top. But it's hard to tell who's "brilliant." Although a family name or a fortune can be passed down from parent to child, the quality of brilliance cannot. Educational credentials are a

poor—but the only—replacement for a name and
wealth in a society where merit appears to be key,
but offers little security. In these circumstances, the
well-educated are motivated to inflate their self-image as "the governing class" and, also, to spread
scorn for the political energy of the "uneducated"—
the middlebrows and lowbrows, the ordinary, the
majority.

The scorn that gets spread finds expression in clichés
that dramatize, then, this powerful strain in our
political sensibility. Consider common character-
izations of politics we all have at the tips of our
tongues. We portray it as a business of "dirty,"
"petty" "pandering" to ignorant voters and selfish
interests. But, at the same time, we say it can be a
"noble profession."[48] What is it that makes the difference? The answer is: leadership. The "noble" leader,
we imagine, must have "the common touch," but
not *be* common. He must have "courage," which we
tend to imagine as strength to stand for "principle,"
"the commonweal," or "sound policy"—therefore,
to stand *against* public opinion, *against* the majority.
We honor his ability to manipulate the electorate in
service of such noble ends. We even go so far as to
tell one another that the people "cry out"—the im-

age of people "crying out" is a revealing one—for such leadership. The people, we want to believe, are desperate to give away their power, to give up government responsive to them; they yearn, we proclaim, for enlightened leaders like *us* to take over.

Yet we don't fully believe it. Insecurity excites us to imagine that the mass of ordinary people, as a brute force, may be on the verge of taking things into their own incompetent hands. Like old colonial administrators, we think we hear drums beating, unseen, in the darkened bush. With an election pending, we worry that it's "a crazy year," it's weird "out there." When incumbents lose office, we say they were "swept out" by a great "wave," a "tide"—a force without face or reason. We gasp about "the tabloids," about "the talk shows," media that seem to engage ordinary people. When citizens, in huge numbers, phone their representatives, we wring our hands over "telephone democracy."[49] Condemning opponents, we charge them with the high crime of stirring up the people, particularly by raising "divisive" issues. Thus Democrats charge that Republicans "divide" us by questioning affirmative action, and Republicans pronounce that Democrats "divide" us by raising issues of class. Our anxiety appears so intense as to make us imagine that around us are traitors—traitors to our very own class, "the governing class."[50]

To the extent that anxiety overcomes us, we shift from our celebration of "noble leaders" to a different form of scorn for ordinary political energy. This involves, on one hand, mockery of political actors, often with knowing irony, often with open delight, putting particular stress on their supposed lack of intelligence. For instance, when then-Vice President Quayle misspelled 'potato', his error inspired weeks of public laughter among the "well-educated class."[51] Along with such mockery of ordinary people in politics there goes, in counterpoint, a grander motif of high-minded disdain. It indulges the fantasy of political narcissism. In this vein, we project ourselves into a government-of-the-imagination—one that transcends politics and ordinary people. We debate state "policy" in sober tones as though it was ours alone to make. With respect, we consider what "thoughtful observers"—that is, one another—recommend. The imaginary process is so refined that we no longer even call it government. We speak, instead, of "governance." What distinguishes the two seems to be that "governance" is a blessedly pure affair, an affair free of any taint by ordinary political energy.[52]

If the dominant sensibility of conventional constitutional discourse is indeed based in these attitudes, why should that move us to imagine ordinary political energy and—in turn—constitutional law any differently? There are two reasons. The first is simply how unattractive we appear when we look in this mirror. If we stop and think about the rancid pomposity of the clichés we repeat and the poses that we strike, imagining we are the governing class, we should be moved to *re*imagine a lot of what we now take for granted. Perhaps a piece of fiction like *Mario and the Magician* can spur us on. Celebrating "noble leadership," we ought to see Cipolla in the mirror. In our mockery of ordinary political actors and our fantasy of "governance," we ought to recognize the self-isolation of the haughty narrator in Mann's story.

But more important is the other reason. It is more practical. It is that the elite attitudes nurturing the sensibility of constitutional discourse are poisonous to our society and our polity. They reinforce a trend, already afoot, of "secession" by "the well-educated," the privileged minority, from intercourse with ordinary people—whether at work or at school or in local communities—that is eroding not only public services and resources, but the very idea of connection among citizens.[53] What is worse, these attitudes reinforce, even inspire, another trend. The disdain felt by elites for ordinary political energy is not, after all, lost on ordinary people. They pick it up from many sources. How can it help, then, but fuel their alienation, much discussed over the past two decades, from the political process—and from government itself?[54] The poison which is spread by the attitudes in question here thus threatens nothing less basic than the legitimacy of our political system, something that, from the viewpoint of constitutional law, ought to matter.

The third (and final) source of resistance to reimagination of the assumptions underlying our discourse about constitutional law is, probably, the most intractable. For it involves an insistence that those assumptions are not just assumptions, but *facts*. This insistence is rooted in the most potent of emotions—fear. And it is supported by the most reassuring of warranties—contemporary consensus, at least among "opinion makers." What it comes down to is a belief that the political energy of the majority of ordinary people is *dangerous,* not simply incompetent, unstable and so on. The belief is that the majority, if given free reign, is prejudiced, intolerant and tyrannical. The belief, further, is that majority power most threatens the most vulnerable of us—nonconformist individuals; racial, religious and other minorities; indeed, any and all "victimized," "disadvantaged," or "unpopular" persons and groups. That this is so is taken to have been demonstrated conclusively, time and again. Why bother, then, even to consider seeing things differently?

In the face of so adamant a conviction, the best that can be done is, first, to pick at its exaggeration and, next, to try redirecting some of its emotional current. This might be undertaken in detail, reaching out to history, sociology, public opinion studies, and the like. Or, it might be undertaken quickly and schematically, seeking to unsettle the settled belief—to open it just enough to let in some fresh air. I am simply going to do that.

To attribute much past or present oppression to "majorities" is, first of all, a ridiculous exaggeration. Majorities rarely rule at all. Certainly, they almost never rule directly. When believers in "majority tyranny" imagine their worst fear, they aren't thinking of a New England town meeting. What they probably have in mind is a mob. But why equate a mob with the majority? Some ordinary people may be in it. In any actual situation, however, many more are not. Indeed, when it comes to engagement in political action, the one thing you can count on a numerical majority to do—for better or for worse—is: almost nothing. Most oppression, then, is the work of *minorities.* And much of it is the work of *elite* minorities—refined, well-educated—whose hands tend, in real life, to clutch the immediate levers of power. Might it not follow that, in order to counter the minorities that oppress vulnerable persons and groups, we should foster—rather than fear—the political energy of a force which might manage to check them: the majority of ordinary people?

But perhaps the fear that drives the belief at issue here isn't really fear of majority *power.* Perhaps, instead, it is fear of political *energy* per se—on grounds that any energetic political activity is very likely to call up the most irrational and most hostile elements in ordinary human nature. Or, perhaps, it is fear of indirect *influence* of majority opinion on the government—on the grounds that ordinary people tend to be deeply prejudiced and intolerant. How might these more plausible convictions be neutralized? The argument most likely to be "heard" is one that speaks to the most essential fear that motivates them—the fear of prejudice.

One especially striking characteristic of both convictions is that they themselves manifest prejudice. They put forth a hostile stereotype. They would make use of the stereotype to repress, on one hand, attempts to shake up the political status quo, and, on the other hand, attempts to make government more responsive to average citizens who lack the means of influence available to more powerful interests. They tend to be held by people who do not imagine themselves to be "ordinary," indeed who imagine themselves as (at least a little) better (at least in some respect) than ordinary. Like most prejudice, that is, they mobilize bias against the stereotyped group, to the advantage of the prejudiced group.

But why view generalizations about supposedly dangerous attributes of ordinary human beings in politics as prejudice rather than as fact? Again, it's the exaggeration that is the tip-off. Whenever an exaggerated generalization mobilizes bias against some other "type" of person—or a "type" of activity by such a person—we should at the very least suspect prejudice.[55] The exaggeration on display here is obvious. Surely, the exertion of political energy is not—in and of itself—incipiently tyrannical. (Think about the Constitutional Convention of 1787.) Nor is the exertion of such energy by ordinary people. (Think of the Revolution or the Abolitionists or the Civil Rights Movement.) When we make sweeping claims about tendencies of majority opinion to intolerance, we display the same kind of exaggeration. When we assume the majority is biased, in fact, we often turn out to be wrong. (Recall the failure of the appeals to anti-gay sentiment at the 1992 Republican Convention.) We frequently dismiss majority opinion as founded on nothing but prejudice—when it plainly is more complicated—simply in order to emphasize our disagreement with it. (Recall the controversy in the early 1970s over busing and "law and order.") Even the most clichéd example of the alleged bias of the majority of ordinary people—the rise of Nazism—is questionable: the Nazis, remember, never won a majority in a free and fair election.[56] Of course, this is not to say that the majority is not often biased. Nor is it to say that it's any less—or any more—prejudiced than the "well-edu-

cated" elites.[57] It *is* to say that such broad claims
about general attributes of ordinary people are biased exaggerations. To the extent, then, that we
reject prejudice, we ought to eschew this one.

What is more, minorities who are themselves ob-
jects of prejudice ought to be able to sympathize
with the majority. For many of the denigrating images projected onto the majority are the very ones
projected onto the minority. Certain racial minorities and women, for instance, know how it feels to
be depicted as childish, irrational, emotional, ignorant, irresponsible, and so on. They ought to be the
last to apply just the same insults to the majority of
ordinary people.[58]

Doing a "Double Take"

Overcoming—or relaxing—your resistance to a re-
imagination of root assumptions of constitutional
law is one thing. Getting you to try such a re-imagination may be another. If you don't know what doing
a double take on ordinary political energy would
mean for constitutional law, you may be reluctant
to do it. You may want a clear idea of the difference
a Populist sensibility would make. But because it is

a sensibility—rather than a set of principles—you simply cannot have it. A sensibility doesn't have "entailments" to enumerate for your inspection.

What I'll do is sketch one way a Populist sensibility *might* inspire us to begin to blaze a path through constitutional argument. It's a path that attracts me. My intention, however, is not to privilege it. Nor am I offering it to invite you to concentrate on details at the expense of everything I've had to say up to now. (We lawyers are all too comfortable befogging fundamentals in disputes over details.) I offer this sketch *only* as a beginning, a very open-textured one. There is lots of room to argue within its outline—just as there is lots of room to argue for blazing different paths inspired by a Populist sensibility.[59] An advantage of approaching constitutional law through issues of sensibility is, indeed, that it keeps us focused on the historical truth that "the law" is no more or less than argument without end. I challenge you, therefore, to press ahead on your own.

To start with, I'll mark out a few precepts. The most basic is a restatement of my exclusion of both the "romantic" and the "counter-culture" perversions of the Populist sensibility. Both would tend to perpetuate distinctions between attributes as "suited" or "unsuited" to active participation in politics—reproducing, in revised form, Anti-Populist repressions of political energy. A distinctive Populist approach, I believe, should make no such discriminations. It ought to favor—subject to limitations implicit in the precept which I'll suggest in a while— the exertion of all sorts of ordinary political energy, "reasonable" or "passionate," "deliberative" or "impulsive," "civilized" or "vulgar."[60]

The second precept has to with what "favoring" all this energy ought to mean. To favor the exertion of political energy isn't to require it. Those who don't participate in political life should not be penalized, since compelled behavior is not exactly a release of energy. Neither, however, should they be insulated in their privacy, protected from exposure to politics. Rather, they should be both *enabled* and *encouraged* to take some part. This implies that they should be given opportunities to take an *effective* part, to get involved in ways that may make some difference.

This implies, in turn, a final precept. Government must not only be responsible to ordinary people. That is not enough. It, above all, must be *responsive* to them—not just occasionally, but systematically, responsive.

Stated so abstractly, these simple precepts may not be too hard to swallow. Once elaborated, they may very well become controversial. For, if generally embraced, they would tend to institute the sort of reorientation of discourse about constitutional law that has occurred, in this century, in the 1900s, the 1930s, and the 1960s—that is to say, more or less, every three decades.

The pivot of this reorientation would be a revised understanding of the central mission, or purpose, of modern constitutional law. Put simply, that mission ought to be to promote majority rule. More fully, the goal inspiring argument about "interpretation" of the Constitution ought to be government of, for, and—to the extent it is feasible—by the majority of the people. Of course, this is simply an ideal. There is no such entity as "the majority."[61] Yet as an ideal, it's no more vaporous than the alternatives. And, at least in its emphasis, it poses a sharp contrast to them. To say the mission of the law is to promote majority rule is not the same as to say it is to protect "individual freedom" or "discrete and insular minorities" *against* "the majority." As an ideal, what is more, it conveys a powerful claim: that "common" people, ordinary people—not their "betters," not somebody else's conception of their supposed "better selves"—are the ones who are entitled to govern our country.

To be sure, affirmation of majority rule has long been a staple of talk about constitutional law. But the power of its simple claim has been sucked out of it. Restoration of that power is the aim of a Populist reorientation of constitutional discourse.

The ideal of majority rule has been sucked dry in two ways. In service of "realism," first of all, the majority has been reduced to coalitions of interest groups[62] ruling at a level removed from much involvement or influence—even from the knowledge— of ordinary people.[63] What is lost, thereby, is attention to broad divisions of social class and status. Lost, too, is attention to the growing frustration of ordinary political energy. In Washington, elite "spokesmen" or "advocates" for interest groups come together and are labelled the "majority." Lost, then, is the critical force of the ideal. At the same time, in service of fantasy, the ideal has been given an apologetic spin. It has been invoked, as I have said, to suggest that ours is—and always has been—a polity in which "the majority rules."[64] So it has fostered a "hiatus"[65] in constitutional discourse. Inspired by the Populist sensibility, however, we can revive the ideal, infusing it with sensitivity to social strata and political energy, sharpening its critical edge. And, recognizing that the majority, so envisioned, does *not* rule, we can turn this ideal of democracy—the mission to pursue it, that is—into the engine of a new era of constitutional activism.

How, then, through constitutional argument, might we criticize failures of majority rule? On what sorts of occasions? Using what sorts of standards? The only answer—anathema to today's academics[66]—is: Who knows? Mapping of legal principle and doctrine is largely a retrospective business,[67] or else it is hubris.[68] What I can suggest are certain general directions that argument might try and certain examples of "settled" issues that ought to be scheduled for an early "unsettling." For further suggestions, and counter-suggestions, I count on you.

A reoriented constitutional argument, promoting majority rule, should concentrate its criticism on behavior—action or inaction—that tends to frustrate opportunity for the effective exertion of ordinary political energy. It should focus not just on government decisions, but on the process that produces, and is produced by, decisions. It should extend its criticism not just to behavior which impedes the summoning and expression of energy, but to behavior which insulates authority from it as well. Thus, if officials set themselves so high "above" ordinary opinion as to fail even to engage with it (think of Mann's narrator), they deserve criticism in the name of the Constitution. If, instead, they engage with it only by manipulating it (think of Cipolla), they deserve the same criticism.

But wait a minute, you say: Such argument, in the name of the Constitution, is way out of bounds. That is true. It is beyond the *present* bounds of argument. This is characteristic of any reorientation of the law—and, as I've said, we have already gone through three reorientations in this century. Yet it's also characteristic of such moments for the orthodox to overstate every departure from established practice. To be sure, in the reorientation I am suggesting, constitutional argument would have to be reshaped to grapple with hard, controversial issues. It would have to gauge the *effects* of official behavior on the political opportunity of ordinary people. It would also have to examine the *politics* behind official behavior. However, constitutional arguments facing up to such questions are not wholly unfamiliar. They have been adumbrated, for example, under the Establishment Clause[69] and the Equal Protection Clause[70] and the guarantee of Freedom of Association.[71] I am suggesting that they be expanded and put to a new use, that they be used to a new, more general and more ambitious end.

Let me suggest a couple, at least, of uses to which they might be put. The reorientation of the law, first of all, ought to encourage the development of novel constitutional claims, some of which have already been made but failed to flourish. Most significant might be frontal challenges to processes of "insider trading"—solicitation of funds, lawyer-lobbying, favors to powerful interests, secret wheeling and dealing— that estrange ordinary people from government.[72] Then, more generally, deference to government in *any* situation might be made to depend on argument about whether the processes that produced the behavior in question deserve deference in fact. That, in turn, might be made to depend not simply on whether the officials knew what they were deciding,[73] but on whether they adequately opened the process to—and responded to—citizens other than professional "spokesmen" and hand-picked "witnesses." Similarly, deference might turn—in the case of referenda, for example—on argument concerning the ways public opinion was manipulated by elites. Such argument, it is clear, would raise issues of definition, fact, and degree, very complex issues. But any more so than those involved in "applying" the Constitution to manage a school system?[74]

A second sort of use to which reoriented constitutional argument might be put involves the ways we evaluate constitutional "rights" of political participation. Animated by a Populist sensibility, we might adjust argument about these issues—rights to vote, to speak, to associate—on three dimensions. Considering basic opportunities for participation, we might skip the usual abstract talk about "the right" to vote or speak and ask how *effective* particular opportunities are for ordinary people.[75] How easy is it for them to get into politics? Is it likely that they can reach relevant audiences?[76] We might even ask: Is the state providing them the "basic" education necessary for effective political participation?[77] Then, considering government regulation of political activity, we might go beyond argument over the weight of "governmental interests" or the neutrality of governmental policy among "points of view." We might argue also about the regulation's *distributive impact on people in different social strata*—insisting, at the least, that the government be neutral in this respect as well.[78] Finally, in talking about rights of political participation, we might focus on what are really the most basic questions: questions of fact. Are the rights *actually being exercised?* By whom? How much? How effectively? Are ordinary people effectively taking part in politics? If not, why not? Paying attention to these issues of fact would, indeed, work a transformation of the practice of constitutional argument about rights.

What drives the Populist approach to rights of political participation is an important adjustment in the imaginative substructure of contemporary argument about them—an adjustment that ought to unsettle a large chunk of the edifice of free speech law in particular. The adjustment is in the image of the sort of person who exercises—that is, whom we like to think of as exercising—freedom of speech. Specifically, constitutional argument seems to have found it hard to imagine ordinary people in that role. It has tended to privilege those modes and styles of expression associated with the "better" sort of people—relatively "reasonable," "orderly," "articulate" speech having "social importance."[79] Indeed, sometimes when an ordinary person's speech is protected, it is belittled. In one of his "great" dissents, Oliver Wendell Holmes called the people he voted to protect "puny anonymities" and argued that a "silly leaflet" posed no danger to anyone.[80] In more recent years, the right to hear *others* speak seems to have been exalted to a status equal to the right to speak oneself—perhaps because it has been assumed that ordinary people need to hear, but need not be heard.[81] (Mann's narrator would certainly embrace such a sentiment.) Of course, there has been a counter-theme in free speech argument.[82] It has, however, been subordinate, and increasingly so. High on a reoriented agenda ought to be a turning of these tables.

Once they are turned—once promotion of ordinary political energy is seen as paramount—several established doctrines will be undermined. The "fighting words" doctrine, for instance, has rested partly on the notion that such words "are no essential part of any exposition of ideas and are of . . . slight social value as a step to truth."[83] This attitude is not simply prissy. What is worse, it may well discriminate against expressions of ordinary energy, "uninhibited, robust . . . wide-open."[84] Another doctrine to be undermined affords special protection to the press, on grounds of its purported "function" as a "surrogate" or a "fiduciary" for the (presumably) passive consuming public.[85] Another radically limits the right of subordinates (workers, students) to speak up to superiors (bosses, teachers) inside hierarchical institutions.[86] Some hierarchical organizations, indeed, might find their own associational freedoms curtailed. Thus the decision upholding suppression of the Communist Party—a decision now widely reviled—might be reaffirmed.[87]

But enough about freedom of speech. What about racial and gender discrimination? Affirmative action? Privacy? Abortion? On these issues, a Populist sensibility may not be perfectly politically correct. To begin with, it does not imagine them as locked in at the absolute center of the constitutional universe. Rather, it would tend to approach them from the perspective of its own central concern—promotion of reinvigorated majority rule. And, from that perspective, it would illuminate issues that lie beneath, and cut across, the ones that recently have dominated constitutional law.

From a Populist perspective, there are no subjects that may be absolutely, categorically, barred from majority rule. In an ideal regime of majority rule, every issue may potentially become a political issue to be resolved, in the first and last instance, politically. Short of the ideal (which is where we are) political regulation of any subject—whether race, gender, privacy, abortion or whatever—ought, at least in the first instance, to face constitutional criticism of a sort no different from the one I've already sketched.

I'll sketch it once more, this time citing two of the great modern arguments for racial equality as models for the two main standards of Populist constitutional criticism. Faced with any official behavior, we should look first at the politics behind it. Specifically, as in *Loving v. Virginia,* we should look to see if this behavior, was generated by an entrenched system of politics whereby certain self-styled "superiors," who occupy positions of power, set themselves above and manipulate or insulate themselves from certain "inferiors." In *Loving,* the system generating the regulation at issue was a system of "White supremacy."[88] Next, we should consider the effects of challenged behavior, its practical effects on opportunity to participate—to promote and defend one's values and one's interests—in majoritarian politics. Thus, as in *Brown v. Board of Education*, we ought to condemn behavior if, in effect, it deprives anyone of something that is basic to opportunity for effective exertion of political energy in "our democratic society."[89] How powerful an argument can be made in these terms to protect, for instance, easy access to abortions, I am not sure. All we can estimate is the extent of the leeway for argument. And, here, it is broad indeed.

Nevertheless, the fact remains that what I am suggesting is a "process-oriented" kind of constitutional argument. Its mission is to improve the democratic process, and, while it is animated by controversial choices of value, this argument does affirm that important controversies ought to be decided through democratic politics.[90] This opens the argument to two criticisms which, I well know, are always on the tips of the tongues of the distinguished inhabitants of legal academia.

First of all, if we have to make certain controversial value choices in constitutional argument, why not make all value choices? If we are to respect the workings of the political process some of the time, but not all of the time, why not pick and choose simply on the basis of our agreement or disagreement with the political winners? To the Populist sensibility, the answer to these questions is clear: For us to claim that *every* value choice ought to be settled through constitutional argument would be to shut out the majority of ordinary people who are not active participants in the process.[91] To see ourselves as so hierarchically "superior" to them—and to ordinary politics—would be to scorn ordinary political energy and the ideal of a reinvigorated majority rule. What is worse, it might well tend to nurture in them a dependence on constitutional law—not just scorning, but sucking away political energy, evoking passivity, inducing enervation.[92]

But, secondly, if that is the case, where do we get off criticizing *anything* that is done through the political process? And, in particular, how can we permit an unelected judge, making constitutional argument, to *order* an elected official around? To a Populist sensibility, this is more troubling than the first criticism. Hence, it deserves a more extended—if less crowd pleasing—response.

Three question-begging answers should be put to one side. First, it is now usual to observe that con-

stitutional argument does, and ought to, go on outside courts and, thus, that it shouldn't be hobbled
by restrictions applicable only to courts.[93] That is
true. But this fails to face the issues that *are* posed
in the judicial context. It is also usual to insist that
judicial power is less problematic if the judges re-
strain themselves by "following" some source of "law"
that is outside themselves. But—as every sophisti-
cated lawyer knows and pretends not to know—
choices among the competing sources of "law" and
among competing implications that may be drawn
from these sources depend on assumptions about
the purpose of constitutional argument, controversial assumptions that, in turn, depend on controversial assumptions about the world in which constitutional argument goes on. At the bottom, as I've
suggested, are opposed sensibilities, neither "correct" or "incorrect." So, the problem remains. Then,
finally, it is usual to claim that judicial power is
tolerable if judges use it to improve the "quality" of
democracy. That is true. It fails, though, to face up
to the fact that "democracy"—and its "quality"—are
fundamentally contested values.

The Populist solution to the problem, I believe, is
to deflate constitutional discourse, to deflate its pre-

tension to argue about, and in the name of, "higher" law. This means affirming—not merely conceding—that what is at the heart of constitutional argument is political controversy about democracy, about what it can be and what it should be. Though the subject is fundamental, the terms of argument about it are not so different from the terms of ordinary political argument. The contending values and interests are the same, even if articulated quite generally. And no fancy "theory," no obsessive "methodology," can hide the fact that, like any argument, constitutional argument appeals—at bottom—to ordinary, competing sensibilities, competing emotions. This affirmation has two virtues. It takes the elitist curse off the practice of argument. And it is true to experience.

The entitlement of judges to take a special part in the making of constitutional argument is a matter—no more and no less—of their job description. It is a job description of long standing. A further entitlement—entitlement to *presumptive respect* for arguments they make—requires a further justification. It can't be based on their being any "better" or more technically "expert" than anyone else. Nor can it be based on their "processes of decisionmaking" being better than any other. Rather, any further entitlement is dependent on two things—the politics of their appointment to the bench and one personal quality: their ordinariness.

By ordinariness, I mean, first, absence of any pretense to lofty status as an oracle of a "higher" law; second, "in tuneness" with what is ordinary in oneself; and, third, a capacity to speak to the ordinariness in others—to all that is shared among all sorts of people. Sheer brainpower, scholarly accomplishments, technical proficiency—that is, most of what are often cited as "qualifications"—are just unessential. By the same token, cleverness, scholarship, and craftsmanship in judicial opinions are also unessential.[94] A couple of decades ago, a United States Senator, protesting such "qualifications," asked whether "mediocre" people don't deserve one seat on the Supreme Court. Revising his thought a bit, I am saying that ordinary people ought not occupy one seat on the Court—they ought to fill all nine. The Court's claim to our presumptive respect depends upon it.[95]

That presumptive respect should turn, also, on the politics of appointment may strike some as troubling. Wouldn't that "politicize" the courts? That is, wouldn't it encourage us to criticize judicial decisions in the midst of political campaigns, seeking to elect candidates who promise to appoint and confirm judges who'll bring to their work the values we embrace? Wouldn't it mean that the general course of constitutional law—the ebb and flow of the assumptions animating it—would tend to "follow the election returns"? The answer is: Yes, that's the whole point. Moreover, it is what has been happening for years—not only in the 1930s, but in presidential elections at least since 1968. From the Populist perspective, this "politicization" of the judiciary—if it can be called that—is not simply familiar, it is vital to whatever authority inheres in the judicial office.

What this point makes clear is that the authority of constitutional argument by judges is defeasible—indeed, it ought to be challenged periodically. Entitled only to presumptive respect, argument by judges, in the end, has to win adherence on its own. It must appeal to ordinary people. It must move them to support it. If they don't, it must adjust and try once more.[96] Does this mean that it's all right not only to criticize or even condemn constitutional argument enforced by judges, but also to disobey it? Again, the answer is: Yes, so long as you're prepared to face up to defeat, and maybe punishment, if the mass of ordinary people fails to support or tolerate your disobedience. Ultimately, the judge and the disobedient dissident are in just the same position—each must try to win over the majority.

By now, I am aware that your Anti-Populist instincts—we all have them, by the way; some of us simply try to control them—may be about to explode in protest. Harsh words—anarchy! nihilism! fascism!—may be on your lips. But hesitate a moment. Consider the banality of what you were about to say. Consider the overheated hyperbole.[97] Affirmation of the value of ordinary political energy and of majority rule surely is not nihilism. To the contrary, it's one powerful strain in the traditional political morality of our nation. And the idea that a Populist sensibility leads to anarchy or fascism depends, first, on images of ordinary political energy that, at the least, are contestable—as I tried to suggest by developing the two takes on *Mario and the Magician.* In addition, it depends on assumptions about the contemporary political situation in our country that are—to be polite—strangely out of touch, even bizarre.

Finally, though, I come to a serious charge. It is

that the Populist sensibility simply "has no place" in constitutional discourse. Why? Because "constitutionalism" and populism are absolutely incompatible. Because the ideas behind the two flatly contradict one another. First of all, the very idea of a constitution is to establish some bedrock restraints on ordinary politics, fixed parameters to channel and check politics. Restraint-by-constitution, moreover, is an idea whose power, whose deep purity, we must preserve. For ordinary political energy is, generally, of terribly low quality and—even if it presents no real threat of anarchy or fascism—very dangerous, at least at retail, as well.

There is no way I can "demonstrate" the second portion of the charge to be unfounded. It is, I have said, a question of sensibility, of one's dominant take on ordinary political energy. All I can do is what I have tried to do—encourage you to do a double take, and then to consider the possibilities of a reorientation of constitutional discourse inspired by a Populist sensibility. If I haven't managed to shake your Anti-Populism, I can only say that I am sorry.

As to the first portion of the charge, I have a sharper answer: Even if you feel a *desire* to believe in "constitutionalism" strong-and-pure, you should recognize that, like so many strong desires, this one can be satisfied only in the clouds of fantasy. There are no supra-political *guarantees* of anything. All there is is politics. Politics already has fundamentally transformed our constitutional law several times in this century, after all. To expect the law to control politics for long, then, is to expect too much. Learned Hand—who certainly would reject much of what I've said—made this point a long time ago:

> I often wonder whether we do not rest our hopes too much upon constitutions, upon laws and upon courts. These are false hopes; believe me, these are false hopes. Liberty lies in the hearts of men and women; when it dies there, no constitution, no law can save it . . .[98]

In this sense, then, constitutions are not incompatible with the idea behind populism. They are *embedded* within it.

For what is behind populism *is* the idea of political liberty: liberty to be shared equally among all, not simply by the "better" people; liberty whose realization demands exercise and requires energy; liberty to shape, then reshape, society.

A few years ago, I saw a photograph taken in Prague of young people carrying through the street a bust of Stalin. Around Stalin's neck they had hung a crude sign. The sign said: "Nothing lasts forever." I put that photo on the first page of my readings for first semester, first year law students. It conveys the first truth about the law.

Does this mean that we ought to have no standards beyond an affirmation of political liberty? That, as citizens, we should agree with—or accept—whatever a reinvigorated majority might do? Of course not. That would be to devalue, even to deny, our own political liberty. The point is to get out and take part in politics ourselves, not looking down from a "higher" pedestal, but on the same level with all of the other ordinary people. That this involves a risk is obvious. We are not sure of victory. We may not even be sure of our own convictions. But such risk is inherent in our Constitution. It is, Holmes said, "an experiment, as all life is an experiment."[99] Politics in a democracy is an unsettling argument, an argument that never will be settled.

The same is true of constitutional law. For there are constitutions. But there is no constitutionalism.

Notes

ᚣ

1. For adumbrations of this approach to constitutional law, see Richard D. Parker, *The Past of Constitutional Theory— And Its Future,* 42 OHIO ST. L.J. 223 (1981) [hereinafter Parker, *Past of Constitutional Theory*]; Richard D. Parker, *Constitutional Voices, in* THE EVOLVING U.S. CONSTITUTION: 1787–1987 (Tung-hsun Sun ed., 1989). The approach will be more fully elaborated in my book to be entitled LAW NOIR: THE POETICS AND POLITICS OF CONSTITUTIONAL ARGUMENT (forthcoming).

2. THOMAS MANN, *Mario and the Magician, in* DEATH IN VENICE AND SEVEN OTHER STORIES (H.T. Lowe-Porter, trans., Vintage International 1989) [hereinafter *Mario*]. Quotations from the story will be from the translation by H.T. Lowe-Porter, originally published in 1936 and now widely available in a Vintage International Edition (1989). The German version was originally published in 1929.

3. MITCHELL COHEN, REBELS & REACTIONARIES 235 (1992).

4. To cite just one example: issues of sexual identity are plainly vital to the story.

5. *E.g.,* PATRICK CAVANAGH, *What's Up in Top-Down Processing, in* REPRESENTATIONS OF VISIONS: TRENDS & TACIT ASSUMPTIONS IN VISION RESEARCH 295 (Andrei Gorea et al. eds., 1991); IRVIN ROCK, PERCEPTION 120–23 (1984); RITA L. ATKINSON ET AL., INTRODUCTION TO PSYCHOLOGY 172 (1990); R.L. GREGORY, EYE AND BRAIN 10–11 (1966).

6. *Mario, supra* note 2, at 133. Rather than having a proliferation of citations for every line I quote, I'll drop a note every few paragraphs to chart my progress through the story.

7. *Id.* at 133–35, 138.

8. *Id.* at 135–37.

9. *Id.* at 137–42.

10. *Id.* at 144–59.

11. *Id.* at 156–64.

12. *Id.* at 166–71.

13. *Id.* at 172–78.

14. *Id.* at 133–35, 139.

15. *Id.* at 135–39.

16. *Id.* at 140–42.

17. *Id.* at 144–45, 153.

18. *Id.* at 147–51.

19. *Id.* at 153–57.

20. *Id.* at 150.

21. *Id.* at 148–59.
22. *Id.* at 160.
23. *Id.* at 154–56.
24. *Id.* at 164–66.
25. *Id.* at 167–71.
26. *Id.* at 169–73.
27. *Id.* at 173–78.
28. *Id.* at 142.
29. *Id.* at 136.
30. Indeed, "socialist realism" [sic] nowadays inspires not simply incredulity, but widespread nausea and alarm as well. To be sure, romanticization of an elite or "vanguard," which sometimes accompanies, as well as contradicts, a "romance of the ordinary," is (I'll claim) *more* nauseating and alarming.
31. Let me note here two important qualifications. First, as I said at the beginning of this lecture, what I am talking about is the cultural effect of the "conventional discourse" of constitutional law. It is the discourse—not the outcomes of cases—that I'm suggesting is bubblelike or repressive. Second, in the book I'm now writing (*see supra* note 1), I'll address the question how a discourse that is bubblelike and repressive can, nonetheless, engage us, "move" us. I won't address that question here.
32. By way of introduction, I'll mention two illustrations—they're no more than anecdotal, to be sure—drawn from my own experience in academic high society. For nearly

ten years, I asked my students to read *Mario and the Magician* for my last class on constitutional law. I found that, for most of them, the first (Anti-Populist) take on the story had clear and consistent priority. And that was after they had listened to me for a semester! Then, just last summer, I asked a group of my faculty colleagues to read it. They, or the few who actually completed the assignment, read it in just the same way. In fact, they (unlike my students) seemed to have great trouble seeing any *other* way to read it.

33. The voting rights and reapportionment doctrines are the exceptions that illuminate the rule.

34. The *Lochner* Court's anguished cry—"[A]re we all . . . at the mercy of legislative majorities?"—could be our cry as liberal or conservative legal "activists" nowadays. Lochner v. New York, 198 U.S. 45, 59 (1905).

35. *See, e.g.,* Adamson v. California, 332 U.S. 46, 59 (Frankfurter, J., concurring), 68 (Black, J., dissenting) (1947). Differences on this point have preoccupied much contemporary argument over the subject. *Compare* ROBERT BORK, THE TEMPTING OF AMERICA (1990) *with* JOHN H. ELY, DEMOCRACY & DISTRUST: A THEORY OF JUDICIAL REVIEW (1980).

36. This account of the amplification of the academic voice in constitutional law is itself a cliché now. Perhaps it is exaggerated, but it is "on to" a vital trend. The next step in this amplification would involve an added accelera-

tion of the tendency to appoint professors to the judiciary.

37. In 1981, I called for just such an enterprise, although I didn't foresee the course it would take. *See* Parker, *Past of Constitutional Theory, supra* note 1.

38. For a brief and interesting review of the last decade's "constitutional theory," see PAUL W. KAHN, LEGITIMACY AND HISTORY 171–209 (1992).

39. Of course, there have been some exceptions. *See, e.g.,* James Gray Pope, *Republican Moments: The Role of the Direct Popular Power in the American Constitutional Order,* 139 U. PA. L. REV. 287 (1990).

40. The same goes for another strain of theory that also focuses on the *quality* of public "dialogue" but doesn't talk about republicanism. For a brief, interesting sketch, see MARK TUSHNET, RED, WHITE, AND BLUE 149–58 (1988).

41. Michael Kelly, *The New Year at a New Age Retreat: The Clintons in Agreeable Company,* N.Y. TIMES, Dec. 31, 1992, at A21.

42. I have heard countless lawyers, as well as non-lawyers, insist that someone with whom they disagree about a question of constitutional law does not "believe in" the Constitution or the Bill of Rights or the First Amendment. The fetishism expressed there is startling if you stop and think about it. For an example of a scholar invoking this sort of fetishism, see Owen M. Fiss, *Objectivity and Interpretation,* 34 STAN. L. REV. 739, 763 (1985).

43. Adam Clymer, *Starring Role In Budget Act: Fear of Voters,* N.Y. TIMES, June 5, 1992, at A9. Ask yourself: Is the Constitution really "the most precious legacy" we can leave to our children? The familiarity of this sentiment may, at first, keep us from appreciating how fetishistic it is.

44. For a comment on "constitutional crisis" rhetoric, see, e.g., Paul Berman, *The Vanities of Patriotism,* THE NEW REPUBLIC, July 1, 1991, at 29.

45. For a very famous example, see Thomas Reed Powell, *Constitutional Metaphors,* THE NEW REPUBLIC, Feb. 11, 1925, at 314.

46. For a wonderful sketch of a vital moment in the modern formation of this attitude—the *Scopes* trial—see GARRY WILLS, UNDER GOD 108–14 (1990).

47. Joseph P. Lash, *A Brahmin of the Law: A Biographical Essay, in* FROM THE DIARIES OF FELIX FRANKFURTER 3, 35 (Joseph P. Last ed., 1975).

48. The ideal image of politics as a "noble profession" has been current at least since the Kennedy administration, with its retrospective, nostalgic, but potent gloss as "Camelot."

49. In the first two weeks of the Clinton presidency, there was a great deal of such hand wringing. *See, e.g.,* Howard Fineman, *The Power of Talk,* NEWSWEEK, Feb. 8, 1993, at 24.

50. Remember the near-hysterical adjectives chosen in 1992— "crazy," "wacko," "wildman"—to dismiss candidates who

were identified as offering strong "populist" appeals to the voters: Ross Perot, Jerry Brown, Pat Buchanan. Then, recall the condemnations of the other candidates (especially, President Bush) who raised issues—"emotional" issues about "values"—that the "governing class" proclaimed (with a bizarre but very familiar self-confidence) were not "the real issues."

51. How do you suppose the laughter struck all the ordinary people who may not be such perfect spellers? Maybe that was the laughter's point. Maybe the mockery was really aimed at ordinary people, and Quayle's offense was to resemble them.

52. Whether or not they're aware of the Leninist origins of the idea, many members of the "well-educated" minority today envision themselves as a sort of "vanguard party," insulated from "the people" who don't know their own "true" interests. This self-image runs through the two versions of disdain for ordinary political energy that I've just sketched—and, in its activist connotation, it may capture the attitude better than the image I've employed, that of a "governing class."

53. For a couple of interesting accounts of the trend, see ROBERT R. REICH, THE WORK OF NATIONS 268–300 (1991); MICKEY KAUS, THE END OF EQUALITY 25–57 (1992).

54. For recent portrayals of this trend, see THOMAS BYRNE EDSALL & MARY D. EDSALL, CHAIN REACTION (1991); E.J. DIONNE, JR., WHY AMERICANS HATE POLITICS (1991).

55. *See* ELY, *supra* note 35, at 157–58.

56. The same goes for the other great disaster (measured in terms of human lives) in our century—the rise to power of Bolshevism.

57. No doubt, "well-educated" elites tend to have different modes of self-presentation, and so might not voice prejudice as the majority does, but does anyone seriously contend that these elites have not, time and again, manifested prejudices of every sort?

58. At a meeting of the Harvard Law School faculty in early 1993, one of my colleagues denounced the harassment of women on the street "by rude blue collar types." He was not aware of the prejudice he was retailing. The voicing of prejudice of that sort, as a matter of fact, is generally unnoticed in such "polite" society. (What if he had said, "rude Hispanic types" or "rude Jewish types"?)

59. The best example is Akhil Reed Amar, *The Bill of Rights as a Constitution*, 100 YALE L.J. 1131 (1991). Because this is a manifesto, not an academic treatise, I do not intend to mention every scholar who has uttered anything relevant to the topic.

60. Thus Bruce Ackerman is partly right about me: I am not what he calls a "dualist." However, as will become clear, I don't fit into the pigeonhole—as a "monistic democrat"—he puts me in either. 1 BRUCE ACKERMAN, WE THE PEOPLE: FOUNDATIONS 9 (1991).

61. At best, majorities form and re-form from time to time and from issue to issue.

62. A *locus classicus* was ROBERT A. DAHL, A PREFACE TO DE-MOCRACTIC THEORY (1956). Citing it, Alexander Bickel reduced majority rule to "'minorities rule.'" ALEXANDER M. BICKEL, THE LEAST DANGEROUS BRANCH 18–19 (1962). Plainly, any group can be divided into any number of sub-groups, delineated by any number of traits. No one line of division is mandated by a law of nature. The question is which traits, and how many of them, we decide to focus on for purposes of constitutional argument—and why.

63. *See* WILLIAM GREIDER, WHO WILL TELL THE PEOPLE (1992).

64. *See supra* text accompanying note 33; *see also* BICKEL, *supra* note 61, at 19.

65. The term is Gordon Wood's, who traces the "hiatus" back to the constitutional rhetoric of the Federalists. GORDON WOOD, THE CREATION OF THE AMERICAN REPUBLIC 1776–1787, at 562 (1969).

66. *See supra* text accompanying notes 36–40. Yesterday's academics, however, understood that doctrine is developed—in activist moments particularly—through a groping, sometimes bold, sometimes cautious, always incremental, imperfect process. *See, e.g.,* BICKEL, *supra* note 61; Jan G. Deutsch, *Neutrality, Legitimacy, and the Supreme Court: Some Intersections Between Law and Political Science,* 20 STAN. L. REV. 169, 188–90 (1968). I like to compare it to the "fog of war." In war, one needs a general *strategy,* but a *blueprint* is, at best, fatuous.

67. John Ely's book is the best contemporary example. ELY, *supra* note 35.

68. For a recent example, see RICHARD A. EPSTEIN, TAKINGS (1985).

69. *See, e.g.,* Edwards v. Aguillard, 482 U.S. 578 (1987); Wallace v. Jaffree, 472 U.S. 38 (1985); Lynch v. Donnelly, 465 U.S. 668, 687 (1984) (O'Connor, J., concurring); Lemon v. Kurtzman, 403 U.S. 602 (1971).

70. *See, e.g.,* Hunter v. Underwood, 471 U.S. 222 (1985); Rogers v. Lodge, 458 U.S. 613 (1982); United States R.R. Retirement Bd. v. Fritz, 449 U.S. 166, 190–91 (1980) (Brennan, J., dissenting); Bullock v. Carter, 405 U.S. 134 (1972); Williams v. Rhodes, 393 U.S. 23 (1968); Harper v. Virginia Bd. of Elections, 383 U.S. 663 (1966).

71. *See, e.g.,* Elrod v. Burns, 427 U.S. 347 (1976).

72. When faced with such suggested arguments, lawyers tend to delay (or avoid) coming to grips with them by focusing on what constitutional provisions such arguments would be "made under." The sort of argument I'm suggesting can comfortably be "made under" the Equal Protection Clause, the Right to Petition Clause, or even the Due Process Clauses. *See* Hans A. Linde, *Due Process of Lawmaking,* 55 NEB. L. REV. 197, 235–51 (1976). Needless to say, Buckley v. Valeo, 424 U.S. 1 (1976)—and its progeny—would be overruled "under" the Free Speech Clause.

73. *See* United States R.R. Retirement Bd. v. Fritz, 449 U.S. 166, 191–93 (1980) (Brennan, J., dissenting).

74. *See* Abram Chayes, *The Role of the Judge in Public Law Litigation*, 89 HARV. L. REV. 1281 (1976). To mention one more example: Argument about term limits for legislators should not focus on wooden assertions about "preemption" or "ballot access" for longtime incumbents. Rather, it should focus on whether such limitations are likely, as a matter of fact, to promote a reinvigorated majority rule.

75. *See* Richard D. Parker, *The Effective Enjoyment of Rights, in* CRITICAL LEGAL THOUGHT: AN AMERICAN-GERMAN DEBATE 485 (Christian Joerges & David M. Trubeck eds., 1989).

76. *See, e.g.,* Clark v. Community for Creative Non-Violence, 468 U.S. 288, 301 (1984) (Marshall, J., dissenting); Perry Educ. Ass'n v. Perry Local Educator's Ass'n, 460 U.S. 37, 55 (1983) (Brennan, J., dissenting); Amalgamated Food Employees v. Logan Valley Plaza, 391 U.S. 308 (1968).

77. *See* Plyler v. Doe, 457 U.S. 202 (1982); San Antonio Indep. Sch. Dist. v. Rodriguez, 411 U.S. 1, 35–37 (1973). The constitutional importance of education from a Populist perspective does *not* have to do with qualitative "improvement" of people, turning (low quality) ordinary people into (high quality) "citizens". Rather, it has to do with provision of resources needed for an effective marshalling of political energy. Needless to say, the question of what resources should be characterized as "basic" for this purpose admits of no "right" or "wrong" answer. But after a decade or two in which expenditure on our public schools has vastly increased and the capacity of the

schools to deliver even minimal skills has collapsed, why don't we see that that presents one of the fundamental constitutional issues of our time? For shocking statistics, *see* ROBERT HUGHES, THE CULTURE OF COMPLAINT 61–67 (1993).

78. *See, e.g.,* FEC v. National Conservative Political Action Commit., 470 U.S. 480, 495 (1985); Kovacs v. Cooper, 336 U.S. 77, 102–03 (1949) (Black, J., dissenting). The (unrealizable but inspirational) ideal might be to extend the one person, one vote principle through all forms of political activity.

79. *See, e.g.,* Young v. American Mini Theaters, 427 U.S. 50 (1976); Spence v. Washington, 418 U.S. 405, 409–11 (1974); Paris Adult Theatre I v. Slaton, 413 U.S. 49 (1973); Brown v. Louisiana, 383 U.S. 131 (1966); Teamsters Union 695 v. Vogt, Inc., 354 U.S. 284 (1957).

80. Abrams v. United States, 250 U.S. 616, 628–29 (1919) (Holmes, J., dissenting).

81. At first blush, focusing on the rights of consumers of speech might appear to foster promotion of the rights of its producers. But, if an audience is described as "captive" or "hostile," its "right" *not* to listen can limit speech. *See, e.g.,* Lehman v. Shaker Heights, 418 U.S. 298 (1974); Public Utils. Comm'n v. Pollak, 343 U.S. 451 (1952); Feiner v. New York, 340 U.S. 315 (1951). More important, and more recently, a focus on the audience has been invoked to frustrate regulations designed to pro-

mote equality in the marketplace of ideas. *See, e.g.,* First Nat'l Bank of Boston v. Bellotti, 435 U.S. 765 (1978). And protection of at least one sort of speech has been *based* on its "value to consumers." *See* Zauder v. Office of Disciplinary Counsel, 471 U.S. 626 (1985). The real significance of the focus on consumption, however, is less operational than as a hint of a shift in the imaginative substructure of argument.

82. *See, e.g.,* NAACP v. Claiborne Hardware Co., 458 U.S. 886 (1982); Cohen v. California, 403 U.S. 15 (1971).

83. Chaplinsky v. New Hampshire, 315 U.S. 568, 572 (1942).

84. New York Times v. Sullivan, 376 U.S. 254, 270 (1964); Terminiello v. Chicago, 337 U.S. 1 (1949). In its analysis of a "fighting words" problem last year, the Court confined itself to consideration of "content" discrimination alone. R.A.V. v. City of St. Paul, 112 S. Ct. 2538 (1992).

85. *See, e.g.,* Richmond Newspapers, Inc. v. Virginia, 448 U.S. 555 (1980); Saxbe v. Washington Post Co., 417 U.S. 843, 850 (1974) (Powell, J., dissenting). Even more egregiously elitist arguments of this sort—for instance, arguments by artists for special protection on "fiduciary" grounds—ought to be aborted before reaching the point of viability.

86. *See, e.g.,* Hazelwood Sch. Dist. v. Kuhlmeier, 484 U.S. 260 (1988); Minnesota Bd. for Community Colleges v. Knight, 465 U.S. 271 (1984); Connick v. Myers, 461 U.S. 138 (1983).

87. Dennis v. United States, 341 U.S. 494 (1951). *See* International Longshoremen's Ass'n v. Allied Int'l, 456 U.S. 212 (1982); Pope, *supra* note 39, at 351–52.

88. 388 U.S. 1, 7–11 (1967). From a Populist perspective, criticism of the politics behind official behavior would be rather different from currently dominant modes of criticism that tend to stress prejudice. Sure, prejudice against a group—any group—would be a consideration, but not, by itself, decisive. Other considerations—actual political leverage, social and economic resources—would tend to be more important. *Cf.* ELY, *supra* note 35, at 135–79. What is more, there might be a tendency to unpack groups defined by race or gender or whatever and focus on social divisions and political inequalities among their "members."

89. 347 U.S. 483, 493–94 (1954). It is worth remembering that the discussion of race in *Brown* was mainly instrumental to the central claim about segregation's devastating effect on social, economic, and, therefore, political opportunity.

90. Though a while back I wrote an article criticizing John Ely's book, which I claimed had "perfected" (a specific kind of) process-oriented argument, I (unlike many other critics) didn't reject process-orientation as such. To the contrary, I looked forward to a revised process-orientation proceeding from open confrontation of controversial issues of value and from a revised imagination of

democracy. *See* Parker, *Past of Constitutional Theory, supra* note 1, at 236–39, 258–59.

91. Ideally, I suppose that the practice of constitutional argument would simply be a dimension of—or a moment in—political controversy among ordinary people. But we should recognize that it has never been that. To romanticize "the people" is to disdain them—and, sometimes, to establish a predicate for rule over them. *Cf.* ACKERMAN, *supra* note 59.

92. Can it be doubted that—until the late 1980s—the prochoice movement's fetishism of *Roe v. Wade* tended to have this sort of enervating, demobilizing effect?

93. I was one of the early ones to make this move. *See* Parker, *Past of Constitutional Theory, supra* note 1, at 259.

94. I'm not suggesting that such qualities are undesirable. All I'm saying is that they are not essential to presumptive respect for judicial constitutional arguments. I should add that, from a populist perspective, we ought to expect judges to write their own opinions and that we ought to applaud the opinions that ordinary people—including judges on lower courts—can readily grasp. This might have the beneficial effect of downscaling the show-off "smartness" of opinions.

95. When I say that, to deserve presumptive respect, judges should be able to "speak to the ordinariness" in others, I don't mean to exclude the capacity for "judgement" or "prudence" or strategic calculation. I simply mean to

deprive those terms of their Anti-Populist overtones and fold them into a deeper and democractic trait. When President Clinton referred to "a big heart" as a qualification for a Justice, he appeared to embrace this idea.

96. This was Alexander Bickel's most important insight into judicial review. BICKEL, *supra* note 61. Unfortunately, out of this simple insight, he—and his many followers— spun an academic fantasy of "dialogue" or "conversation" (even of a "seminar") among "the people" and the Court. For a recent and fascinating book in the tradition inaugurated by Bickel, see ROBERT A. BURT, THE CONSTITUTION IN CONFLICT (1992).

97. Apparently, many writers in our "dignified" field don't stop to control themselves. In the past several years, I've been called a "nihilist," ROBERT F. NAGEL, CONSTITUTIONAL CULTURES: THE MENTALITY AND CONSEQUENCES OF JUDICIAL REVIEW 125 n.19 (1989), and a "revolutionary," BORK, *supra* note 35, at 207 (1990).

98. LEARNED HAND, THE SPIRIT OF LIBERTY 189–90 (1952).

99. Abrams v. United States, 250 U.S. 616, 630 (1919).